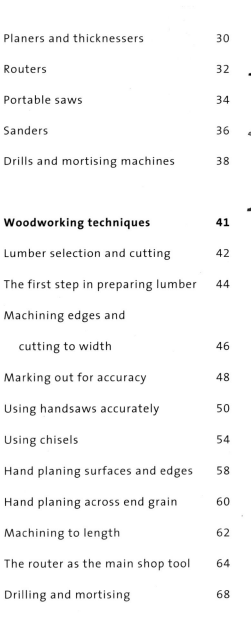

Introduction

WOOD is one of the most beautiful and versatile materials known to man, and working with it is a truly satisfying pastime. Before that can happen, however, the beginner needs to learn how to use, sharpen and care for the basic range of hand tools, as well as how to use small power machines safely and competently. Once you are familiar with the more common woodworking tools, you can learn the necessary techniques – from the basic preparation of lumber and sawing of it into smaller components to more advanced woodworking techniques such as routing and shaping.

Do not be tempted to bypass hand tools and move straight to the promise of the quick, accurate result given by power tools and machines. You would be casting away the great pleasure of working in a calm, quiet, dust-free workshop, creating silky plane shavings and controlling joints created accurately with hand tools you have learned to keep razor-sharp. The skills required to recondition, sharpen and use planes, chisels and saws are relatively easily acquired. They do take a little patience and time but the rewards are immeasurable.

When you do progress to using power tools, you will find there are two distinct categories in a home workshop: hand-held or portable power tools such as finishing sanders, drills and routers, and fixed power tools or machines. Some tools fall into both categories, for example the portable circular saw that can, if turned upside down and fitted beneath a machine table, be turned into a stationary machine. Always remember that when you use a power tool or machine in your workshop at home, it is your responsibility to ensure your own safety and you would be well advised either to seek advice on the subject from a competent professional woodworker or to attend a short course on the subject.

Above *This placing of the table saw and band saw best uses the space in this light, airy workshop*

Left *The joy of using hand tools with a good sturdy workbench*

Hand and power tools

THE HOME WOODWORKER will need a basic assortment of hand and power tools to hand. Other equipment will be required only infrequently for specific tasks. The hand tools and small machine tools on the following pages are those most commonly found in the small workshop. Whenever buying tools, especially hand tools, always buy the very best you can afford. A good hand tool will last more than one lifetime and, quite often, second-hand tools offer very good value for money. Buy tools as you need them rather than because you feel you should have them. Many professional craftspeople own a relatively small selection of tools but use all of them to great effect.

Measuring and marking tools

ACCURACY IS REALLY a very simple matter. Taking great care, mark out your components exactly to size and then, again taking great care, cut precisely to your marking line. This way your components cannot help but fit exactly together. This process begins with accurate, clean, marking out – starting first with marking knives.

Marking knives

These are used in preference to pencils for marking out because, whereas a pencil line has a thickness, a marking knife is bevelled on one side only and is therefore capable of giving a mark of absolute accuracy. Sharpen your marking knife as carefully as you would a chisel and buy the best available. The steel should be of exceptional quality as it has to be rubbed constantly against the steel blades of squares and rules.

Above *Different types of marking knives; craftspeople's preferences vary greatly and selection is a personal choice*

Gauges

Marking and cutting gauges are used to scribe dimensions with the grain and across the grain, respectively. A marking gauge is fitted with a small sharp pin, while a cutting gauge is fitted with a small scribing knife, again sharpened with a bevel only on one side like a marking knife. You may need two or three gauges since occasionally it may be necessary to leave a gauge set to a particular dimension for a period of time. You may choose to have both types of gauge, but standard marking gauges can be adjusted to work well both with the grain and across it.

Mortise gauges are fitted with two pins, one of which is adjustable to enable parallel

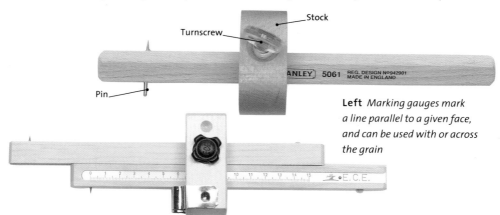

Turnscrew — Stock

Pin —

ANLEY) 5061 REG. DESIGN Nº942901
MADE IN ENGLAND

Left *Marking gauges mark a line parallel to a given face, and can be used with or across the grain*

lines to scribe the position of mortise-and-tenon joints. You will find that you need a mortise gauge – it is an important tool and it is worth getting the more expensive but easier-to-use versions of this tool where the

second, movable, pin is controlled by a screw thread.

Rules and edges

The dimensions of woodworking projects are checked against workshop rules. Rules are divided into inches or millimeters. Some have both

measurements. It is useful to have a 24–inch rule kept by the bench and a 6-inch rule, which can fit in an apron pocket. A retractable tape measure is often used for larger components but is much less accurate than a big steel rule.

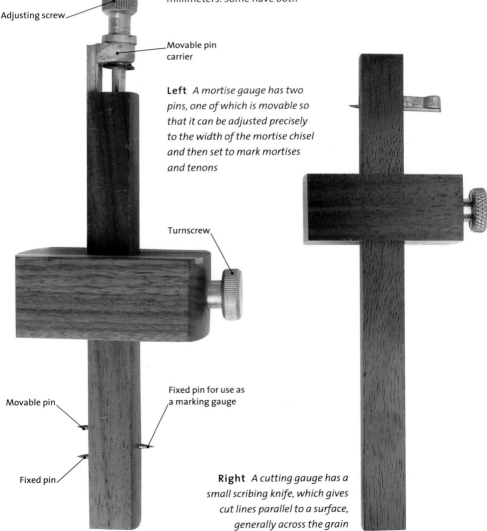

Adjusting screw

Movable pin carrier

Left *A mortise gauge has two pins, one of which is movable so that it can be adjusted precisely to the width of the mortise chisel and then set to mark mortises and tenons*

Turnscrew

Movable pin

Fixed pin for use as a marking gauge

Fixed pin

Right *A cutting gauge has a small scribing knife, which gives cut lines parallel to a surface, generally across the grain*

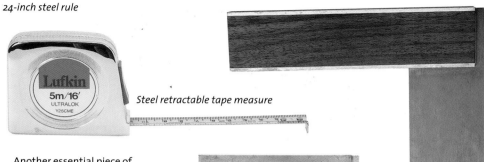

24-inch steel rule

Steel retractable tape measure

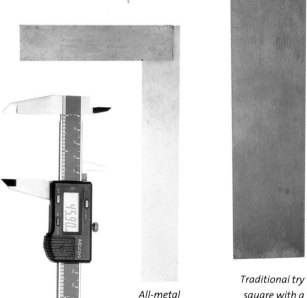

Another essential piece of equipment is a straight edge, about 40 inches long. This is used to check components and other tools for flatness. Do not rely on the edge of a rule to do this job as it may not be as straight as you need it to be.

Dial calipers are wonderful tools and have many uses within the workshop – principally checking the thickness of components. A less expensive, plastic dial caliper measuring to 1/100 inch is easily accurate enough for woodwork and has the benefit of not suffering unduly if dropped.

Squares and sliding bevels

A combination square comprises a short rule that accepts a number of different heads, such as a protractor or a 90°, 45° and spirit level head. It is very useful but can be heavy and cumbersome and, unless of very good quality, can lead to inaccurate work. Sliding bevels are used for

All-metal engineer's square

Traditional try square with a steel blade and brass-faced lumber stock

Left *Vernier gauge, for very accurate measuring; can be read from a dial scale or a digital readout. The extending pin acts as a depth gauge*

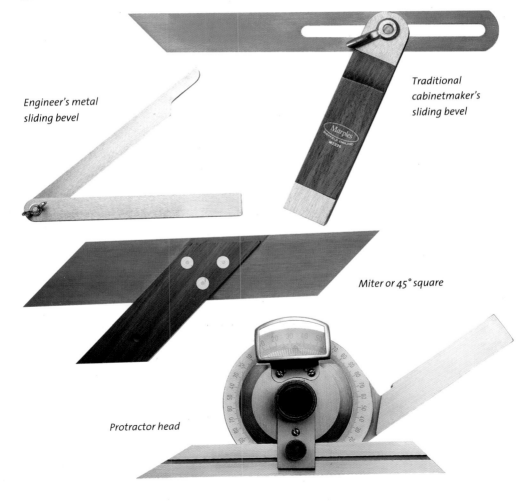

33 34 35 36 37 38 39 40 41 42 43 44 45 46 47 48 49 50 51 52 53 54 55 56 57 58 59 60 61

13   14   15   16   17   18   19   20   21   22   23   24

marking out angles. Where possible, use an all-metal engineer's sliding bevel. Marking templates for dovetail joints can also be used, but attractive brass templates should be avoided since the steel

marking knife can wear the brass template very quickly.

A square that is not quite square is a traitorous implement in the workshop. Where possible, use good-quality all-steel engineer's squares. A

small 6–inch square and a 2-inch square are perfectly adequate for most work. Wooden-handled, steel-bladed squares are perfectly adequate for rough, large-scale work where accuracy is less critical.

Engineer's metal sliding bevel

Traditional cabinetmaker's sliding bevel

Marples

Miter or 45° square

Protractor head

Handsaws

CROSSCUT SAWS and ripsaws are bench saws that have their teeth sharpened in two different ways. The leading edge of a crosscut tooth slopes away from the vertical, while a rip-tooth leading edge is vertical. In addition, a crosscut tooth is filed at an angle to its face and a rip tooth is at 90° to its face. The teeth of the crosscut saw act like knives severing the wooden fibers, whereas the teeth of a ripsaw act like tiny chisels paring material away in their progress down the grain of the lumber. A crosscut saw is essential for work on damp softwoods, but the ripsaw is more useful with dry hardwoods, and many cabinetmakers reset their fine-tooth panel saws with a rip-tooth configuration. Man-made boards like MDF and chipboard will dull a handsaw very quickly, so for these boards use an inexpensive hardpoint saw that cannot be resharpened.

A high-quality bench saw will have a tapered ground blade that is thicker near the teeth and thinner near the top. This gives relief to the cut and helps to guide the saw as you work. A small panel saw with 10 TPI (teeth per inch) would be a useful bench saw if you were not using many machines in the workshop.

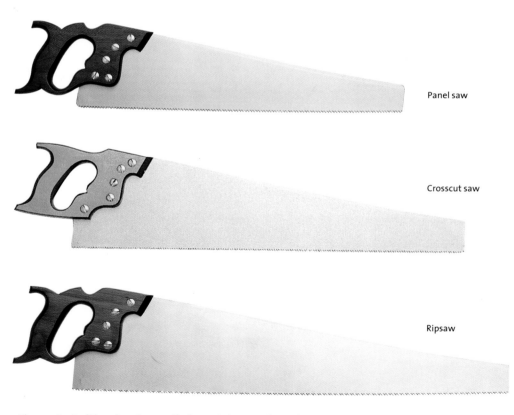

Panel saw

Crosscut saw

Ripsaw

Above *A set of three bench saws, the longest sharpened as a ripsaw to cut along the grain, and the medium one as a crosscut saw for cutting across the grain; the smallest one is a general-purpose panel saw*

Backsaws

Another commonly used saw is the backsaw. This has a stiff brass back and comes in two sizes: the tenon saw and the dovetail saw. In common with most new tools supplied today, backsaws invariably need some reconditioning in order to perform properly. In this case, the layer of varnish that is usually applied to the blade must be removed, as must some of the set applied to the saw teeth, using either a small slip stone or a tiny hammer and tapping very gently against a small anvil. The set is applied to the teeth so as to make the saw cut a groove or "kerf" wider than the plate of the saw. This is a good reason for making sure that your saw has some set, but quite often this kerf is wider than necessary. By reducing the kerf of the new saw you reduce the energy and work required to use the saw and thereby

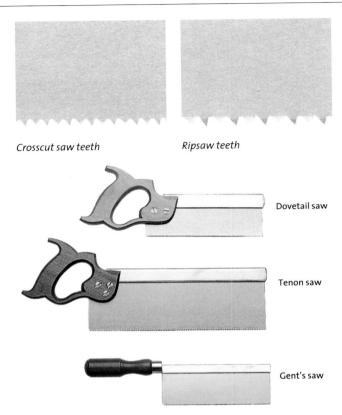

Crosscut saw teeth   *Ripsaw teeth*

Dovetail saw

Tenon saw

Gent's saw

Above *A set of three backsaws: a dovetail saw, a tenon saw and a very fine gent's saw*

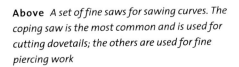

Coping saw

Adjustable frame or bow saw

Fixed frame or bow saw

Above *A set of fine saws for sawing curves. The coping saw is the most common and is used for cutting dovetails; the others are used for fine piercing work*

increase your control over it. Most craftspeople would have two or three backsaws: a tenon saw for general work and larger joints, a small 8-inch dovetail saw with very little set on it for small joinery, and a 10-inch dovetail saw or a smaller tenon saw for larger carcasses.

Other types of saw

Japanese saws are popular; they are beautifully sharpened from new and cut a very thin and fine kerf. One disadvantage is that, unlike most Western saws, they invariably cut on the pull stroke rather than on the push stroke.

Piercing and coping saws are popular for some small curved work, and the gent's saw, named after the Victorian gentleman woodworker, can be used for small delicate work. However, it is no substitute for a well-set dovetail saw. Finally, the miter saw is a modern frame saw set in a jig so as to cut at predetermined angles. This is popular for picture-framing and for cutting small components true and square.

Sharpening saws

It is possible to sharpen all your saws in the workshop, although it is not to be recommended. Saw sharpening specialists have the equipment and expertise to sharpen bench saws much more accurately than even a skilled hand can do. What you can do yourself, however, is sharpen the very small saws. Dovetail saws are best sharpened using a 4-inch Swiss precision saw file held at right angles to the blade. The technique is to settle the file into the gullet of each tooth and to give one stroke to each tooth. Sharpen saws like this little and often, rather than waiting for them to become dull and useless.

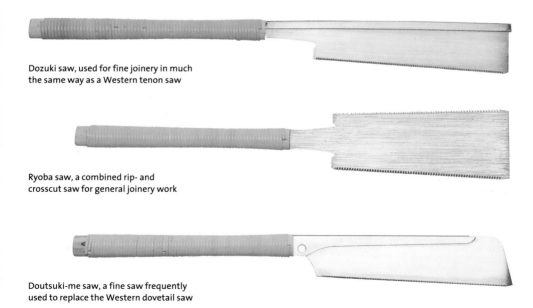

Dozuki saw, used for fine joinery in much the same way as a Western tenon saw

Ryoba saw, a combined rip- and crosscut saw for general joinery work

Doutsuki-me saw, a fine saw frequently used to replace the Western dovetail saw

Above *Japanese saws have become popular additions to the woodworker's tool kit. They have very fine blades and generally cut on the pulling action*

Above *Modern frame miter saw*

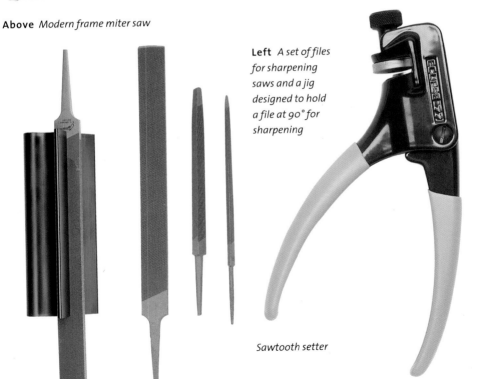

Left *A set of files for sharpening saws and a jig designed to hold a file at 90° for sharpening*

Sawtooth setter

Chisels

BEVEL-EDGED CHISELS will be some of the most important hand tools you possess. Much of your work with chisels will be done with ones ranging in size from ¼ inch (6 mm) to ¾ inch (19 mm). There will be some occasions when you need wider bench chisels or paring chisels but these are few and far between. So, if you are buying chisels for the very first time, go for a beautiful set of small chisels and get the feel of using and sharpening them before moving to larger, more expensive tools. Rather than have a complete set of chisels, many craftspeople rely on a collection of small chisels less than ½ inch wide. Unless they work regularly on large projects they might have only three other larger chisels of differing widths up to about 1¼ inches.

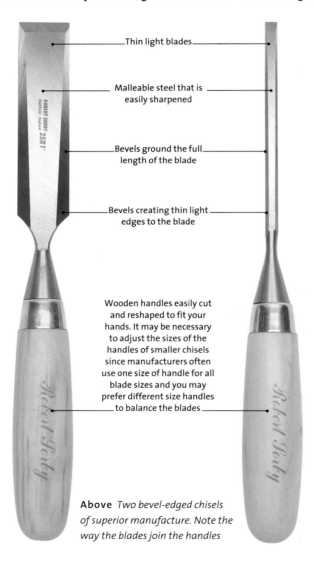

Thin light blades

Malleable steel that is easily sharpened

Bevels ground the full length of the blade

Bevels creating thin light edges to the blade

Wooden handles easily cut and reshaped to fit your hands. It may be necessary to adjust the sizes of the handles of smaller chisels since manufacturers often use one size of handle for all blade sizes and you may prefer different size handles to balance the blades

Above *Two bevel-edged chisels of superior manufacture. Note the way the blades join the handles*

Tool selection

Choose a range of chisels that fits and becomes an extension of your hands. Chisel handles should balance the weight of the blade, i.e., small handles for small sizes and larger handles on wider chisels. This, together with the way the blade is shaped, is more important than the hardness of the steel that forms the cutting edge. Although there are immense benefits to be gained from buying Japanese chisels in the larger sizes, many craftspeople prefer European chisels in the smaller, more delicate sizes. European tools are lighter, and easier and quicker to sharpen than Japanese tools. The latter have laminated cutting edges, which means that they have harder steel at the cutting edge. Therefore, if used properly, Japanese chisels hold their edges several times longer than their European counterparts. Larger Japanese chisels also benefit from the Japanese practice of hollow grinding chisels, which allows the user to get the back of the chisel perfectly flat and mirror polished.

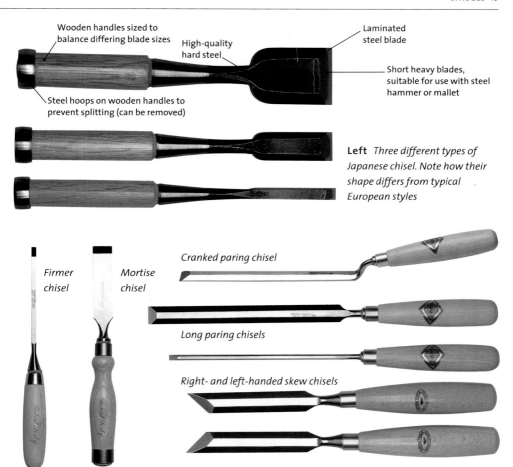

Wooden handles sized to balance differing blade sizes

High-quality hard steel

Laminated steel blade

Short heavy blades, suitable for use with steel hammer or mallet

Steel hoops on wooden handles to prevent splitting (can be removed)

Left *Three different types of Japanese chisel. Note how their shape differs from typical European styles*

Firmer chisel

Mortise chisel

Cranked paring chisel

Long paring chisels

Right- and left-handed skew chisels

Heavier, square-sided, firmer chisels and mortise chisels are also available but are not really widely used by the modern woodworker. Bevel-edged paring chisels of ⅝-inch (15–mm) and 1¼-inch (30–mm) widths are useful for fine, delicate work and should never be struck with a mallet or hammer. There are two or three other chisels that you may need to find a budget for. The first

would be a matched pair of left- and right-handed skew ground chisels. These are essential tools for clearing out the corners of lapped dovetails – most commonly found on the front of drawers. You can clear those few corner fibers away with a bench knife but a skew ground chisel is a much better tool. It is possible to buy left- and right-handed skew ground chisels from a good tool supplier but you could take

the opportunity of finding a useful purpose for one or two of your spare chisels (or buy some from a second-hand shop) and grind them for yourself.

Lastly, a cranked paring chisel is very useful for cleaning out the inside of assembled carcasses. It is almost impossible to slice off those tiny knobs of half-dried glue that squeeze out of a joint without the assistance of a cranked paring chisel.

Planes

ONE OF THE most essential operations in furniture-making is ensuring the surface is flat, straight and true. This is carried out by planing, which is in itself a skill in woodworking that is a pleasure to develop and very satisfying when competence has been achieved.

Bench planes

Bench planes are used by most woodworkers to prepare surfaces prior to final finishing and to trim and fit joints. There is enormous satisfaction to be gained from using a well-adjusted plane accurately to take off those one or two shavings that turn a tight uncomfortable joint into a perfect fit.

Bench planes are generally available in three or four lengths: the short smoothing plane, the intermediate jack and fore planes and the long jointer, or try, plane. Planes developed this way in order to perform different functions. Before machines took on the laborious task of planing rough boards into flat, dimensioned lumber, a woodworker would have needed a full set of planes: a jack plane for initial preparation, a fore plane for final truing up, a jointer plane for straight-edged joints and, finally, a smoothing plane to true off assembled carcasses. Most woodworkers today manage with one jack plane of medium length and a smoothing plane. Wooden planes are very popular, being easier to tune and set up, and lighter and nicer to use than their metal counterparts.

Specialist planes

Specialist planes like block planes and shoulder planes are a distinct category of tools, different from the bench planes but none the less very useful small tools. Block planes can be used both with and across the grain. They have a low cutting angle and an adjustable mouth, which makes them very versatile tools. Unlike the larger bench planes described above, block planes and some of the other specialist planes have their blades set at a low cutting angle

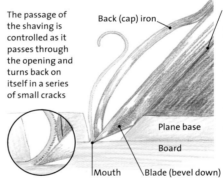

The passage of the shaving is controlled as it passes through the opening and turns back on itself in a series of small cracks

Back (cap) iron

Front face of frog.

Adjusting the frog forward or backward allows control of the position of the cutting edge in relation to the mouth, i.e., a wide mouth setting for coarse work and a narrow mouth setting for fine work and interlocking grain

Plane base

Board

Mouth   Blade (bevel down)

Above *Cross-section of a hand plane in use*

Below *Wooden smoothing plane*   Blade

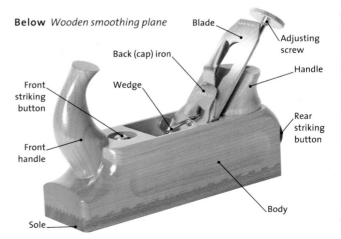

Back (cap) iron

Front striking button

Wedge

Adjusting screw

Handle

Rear striking button

Front handle

Sole

Body

Throat adjustment lever

Adjustment wheel

Metal casting

Sole

Toe

Block plane for planing end and difficult grain

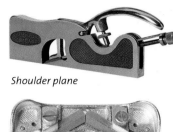

Shoulder plane

Side rabbet plane

in the body of the plane, probably between 10° and 20°. This low cutting angle is combined with setting the blade in the body of the plane with the bevel up. This bevel-up configuration gives an overall cutting angle similar to the 45° of bench planes, because the 15° that the iron is set in the body of the plane is added to the blade sharpening angle of 30°. The benefit of this is that it enables planes designed with the bevel of the cutting iron facing upward to be modified, simply by

grinding and honing the cutter to a different angle in order to change the overall cutting angle. This is especially useful when planing boards with wild grain configurations.

Shoulder planes are designed similarly but, in addition, have a blade the full width of the body, which enables them to cut right into the corner of a joint such as a rabbet or the shoulder of a tenon. Many woodworkers find that owning one large and one small shoulder plane enables them to do most kinds of work.

The side rabbet plane is a plane that you would need perhaps only once every two years or so, for example to enlarge just fractionally a groove that accepts the edge of a panel. But on that one occasion it would be impossible to do the job with anything else.

Plane blades

Plane blades come in two distinct forms. Block and shoulder planes have their blade set at a low cutting angle and with the bevel of the blade facing upwards. Conventional bench planes come with a high 45° cutting angle and with the bevel of the blade facing downwards and a back iron fitted to the rear of the blade. The back iron is positioned close to the cutting edge and is there to help control the path of the shaving through the mouth of the plane and prevent tears and splits in the shaving. It is very important that the back iron is fitted carefully to the blade to enable it to function properly.

Below *Metal jack plane*

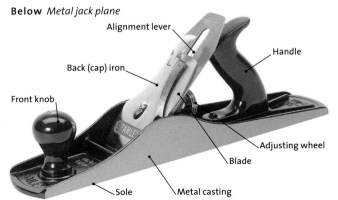

Alignment lever

Handle

Back (cap) iron

Front knob

Adjusting wheel

Blade

Sole

Metal casting

Reconditioning edge tools

RECONDITIONING IS THE PROCESS of preparing a tool or an edge tool prior to sharpening. Although laborious work, it is usually done only once in the lifetime of the tool. It is a process of upgrading the tool to a level of precision and function that the manufacturer cannot economically provide. In the case of chisels, this is done by working on the back of the blade to provide a flat true surface that has been worked to a high mirror polish. When completed, the back of your chisel should only ever touch the finest polishing stone.

Reconditioning chisels

First your blade must be checked for flatness. This is important because a truly flat blade is easier to sharpen. This process is achieved with a flat steel lapping plate and carborundum powder, lubricated with either water or oil. (A less expensive alternative to the steel lapping plate is a piece of plate glass with ground edges.)

Rub the back of the chisel on the flat lapping plate with this abrasive to check for an even gray color right out to the edges and corner of the chisel. Be careful to incorporate all of the carborundum as you work since this abrasive breaks down with use to give a finer and finer finish, and any coarser grains left will scratch the surface of the blade you are trying to set true. Once a true surface has been created – this takes about 15 minutes with a ½-inch (12–mm) chisel – you can check your work by polishing the back of the chisel first on a 1000 grit Japanese water stone, lubricated with water, and finally on a 6000 grit polishing stone. If an even polish does not come up very quickly, go back to the carborundum plate. There is no point attempting to use a water stone to flatten your edge tools – these are polishing and sharpening stones and will not alone produce a flat surface. Be very careful not to get carborundum paste on the Japanese water stones. Your objective should be a finely polished surface right across the cutting edge and right out to the corners of the chisel –

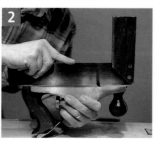

RECONDITIONING A PLANE BLADE

1 Securely tape a length of 60 grit abrasive paper to a machine table or other protected flat surface ready for reconditioning your plane. Rub the sole of the plane along the abrasive paper.

2 Ensure the sole is perfectly flat by checking it against a straight edge.

3 Hold the plane up to the light to see if the polished surface is precisely flat.

4 It is essential to ensure that

bear in mind that it is the corners of the chisel that do the most effective work.

If working on Japanese chisels, note that these wide and extremely hard tools have hollow ground undersides, which make the preparation and reconditioning of these chisels much easier. Without this hollow grind the preparation of these chisels would take a very long time indeed.

Reconditioning planes

Steel planes must also be reconditioned before they will work effectively. The sole of a plane is almost never flat and true when new. Use a roll of 60 grit abrasive paper on a flat machine table to lap the sole of your plane

true and flat. This can be checked by using a straight edge and looking against a strong light source. This process may have to be repeated once or twice in the first year while the plane's casting continues to move; after some time it does eventually settle down.

Having flattened the sole, next adjust the frog of the plane. This is the steel block upon which the blade assembly sits. Check the fit of the frog to the plane body and, if necessary, file the frog to fit tightly.

Next, check that the blade assembly fits similarly closely to the frog. Finally, slide the frog and blade assembly backward and forward until the gap in front of the cutting edge is approximately 1/16 inch wide;

then locate the frog and tighten the adjustment screws. This will help the plane cut more effectively, preventing tear-out with "difficult" species of hardwood.

For a bench plane to function properly the blade will need to be slightly curved across its width. This is to encourage the blade to cut a shaving with a width of only approximately 1 to 1 3/8 inches in the middle of the blade. The back iron, which fits on the back of the cutting iron, should be filed and adjusted to fit cleanly upon its mate. There should be no gap between these two pieces of steel, otherwise shavings will get jammed between them. The front surface of the back iron should also be polished to present a smooth surface to any shaving.

the back iron is adjusted to fit closely behind the cutting edge of the plane so that no shavings can pass beneath the back iron.

RECONDITIONING A CHISEL
5 Reconditioning the back of a chisel on a polishing stone finishes an even polish.

Sharpening edge tools

SHARPNESS IS ESSENTIAL in order to achieve control over a tool's cutting edge. It is a means of reducing the force or power required to push that edge through the lumber. The more power you require to shove your plane across or push your chisel through the lumber, the less control you have. If the tool's edge is sharp, it will slice through with the minimum of effort; if it is dead blunt you will have to shove and push and force and struggle your way through the wood. So keep your tools sharp and be sensitive as to how their edges are performing. If you sense any slight increasing resistance in a tool, hone the cutting edge. Never let a blade become blunt; always touch it up well before it reaches that stage.

Grinding

Sharpening, or honing, is achieved by first using a water-cooled grinder to create a bevel of 25°. Water-cooled grinders are easy to use and the coolant prevents the cutting edge from overheating and burning in the grinding process. Burning the cutting edge "draws the temper," or changes the hardness of the cutting edge, and can ruin a good and expensive tool in less than a moment. It is important to be able to regrind your tools easily, so it is worth spending a generous part of your budget on a good water-cooled grinder. It is possible to buy relatively inexpensive edge tools and chisels; sharpen them frequently before they lose their edge, and they will function as well or better than the most expensive hand-made laminated edge.

Honing chisels

After grinding, the next step is to use the honing stones. These are synthetic stones made in Japan and lubricated with water. There are other systems but Japanese water stones are cheaper, quick to use and produce a superb edge. You will need two stones – one of 1000 grit and the other a polishing stone of 6000 grit. To hone an edge, rest the chisel on the honing stone with the bevel side down. Press down on the back of the chisel so the cutting edge is in contact with the stone and the chisel is also supported on the flat surface of the stone by the other end of the hollow ground surface created on the grinder. Having settled the chisel on the surface of the stone, carefully pull the chisel back towards you. Use a honing guide for this if you wish. Your objective is to hone the front $3/64$ inch of the cutting edge.

After two or three strokes on the honing stone you will see a small burr created along the cutting edge. Move to the polishing stone and by working on alternate sides of the chisel polish the edge until that burr falls away. Watch for the burr to fall away completely; do not strop it or remove it with a finger. Polish it away and you will then have a perfect, sharp cutting edge.

Left A combined water-cooled grinder and hard rubber wheel for polishing

Left Japanese water stones in a unit that lubricates and stores the stones

HONING PLANE BLADES

1 You can use a honing guide when honing a chisel or a plane blade. The honing guide holds the blade at the correct angle in relation to the stone.

2 With practice, however, you will find that you can hone tools without needing the guide.

3 Plane blades before honing (left) and after honing (right).

CHISEL BLADES

4 This shows the burr that has developed on a chisel that is being honed.

5 Here, the burr has been polished away to produce a very sharp cutting edge.

USING A GRINDER

6 A turning gouge is being ground on a grinding wheel. The heat builds quickly so take care not to burn your tools when grinding. It is not recommended to grind carbon steel cutting tools on a bench grinder.

Clamps

IT IS ONE of the secrets of woodworking that when two or more pieces of wood are glued together to make a good tight joint, it is necessary to apply a little bit of pressure and hold the job there while the glue sets. This is done by applying clamps.

The different types available

All-metal C-clamps are available in several sizes and depths and can be used to apply enormous amounts of pressure, invariably more pressure than you will need. A well-made joint simply needs a little bit of glue and a little bit of squeeze. What you do need, however, is consistent pressure all along the joint, which may mean that you need 10 or 12 clamps for one small assembly job.

One of the benefits of the wooden cam-action clamps is that although they are not suitable for applying high pressure, they are easy to use and very light in weight. This type of clamp is also relatively inexpensive.

The main type of workshop clamp is, however, an all-metal fast-acting clamp. Although these clamps are the best available for fast assembly work in a busy workshop they can be expensive.

Single-handed clamps are useful in situations where it is necessary to apply the pressure while holding the work in one hand and tightening the clamp in the other. Apart from this undoubted advantage this type of clamp is not really robust enough to withstand heavy use.

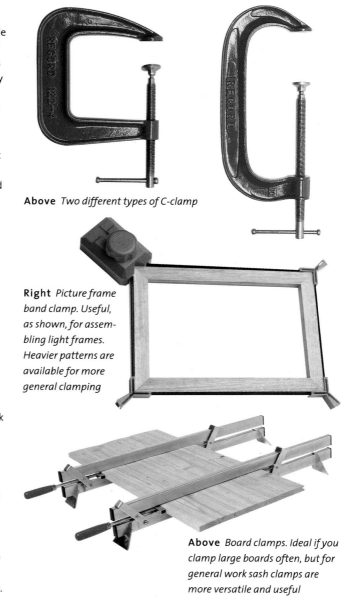

Above *Two different types of C-clamp*

Right *Picture frame band clamp. Useful, as shown, for assembling light frames. Heavier patterns are available for more general clamping*

Above *Board clamps. Ideal if you clamp large boards often, but for general work sash clamps are more versatile and useful*

Above *Wooden cam-action clamp. These can have a fixed end or two movable cam-action heads, as here. Useful for light holding*

Right *Fast-acting clamp. Buy good-quality ones since they can easily be over tightened and ruined if substandard or abused*

Sash clamps, with either a thin light bar or a heavier T-section, are the most widely used method of jointing boards together to form panels. Called sash clamps because of their original use in the clamping of windows and door frames, these would typically be used with two or three clamps beneath the panel and two or three clamps above, placed at distances of 4–6 inches apart. The lighter section sash clamps are adequate for small jobs, especially if they are high-quality ones, but for general workshop use and large work the heavy T-section clamps are recommended. Always keep the bars of sash clamps well waxed and free of any glue that might squeeze out; and protect the job from the jaws of the clamp by using a clamping block or wooden spacer. Again, when clamping any work, remember the maxim: a well-made joint requires but a small amount of pressure and a small amount of glue. If you have to apply excess pressure to bring the joint together then something is wrong.

You can never really have enough clamps. Start off with perhaps six clamps and buy more as the need arises. Beginners may find the new single-handed clamps very useful. There are some very cheap clamps available that may do the job if your budget is limited, but assembly tools are important tools, so do get the best that you can afford.

Left *Sash clamps – rectangular and T-bar. The traditional clamp for cabinet assembly work and still one of the best. Rectangular sectioned ones are fine for light work, but T-bars are useful when extra pressure is needed*

Hammers and screwdrivers

SCREWDRIVERS AND HAMMERS join clamps and clamps in the category of assembly tools. There are many aspects of cabinetmaking where clamps should not be used, for example when assembling a drawer. A drawer would instead be "knocked up." This would be done using either a small nylon-faced hammer or even a small steel-faced hammer, and you would choose the size of the hammer to suit the size of the job in hand.

Hammers

One of the most useful tools for assembling large dovetail carcasses is a 4–pound club, or lump, hammer, frequently used by builders for demolition. This tool is used to drive the joint together and expel the last bit of partially dried glue left in the corner of the joint.

Nylon-faced or rubber-faced hammers are frequently used in preassembly work because they do not mark the surface of the job. These soft-faced hammers are, however, often replaced in the final gluing with a steel-faced hammer because the

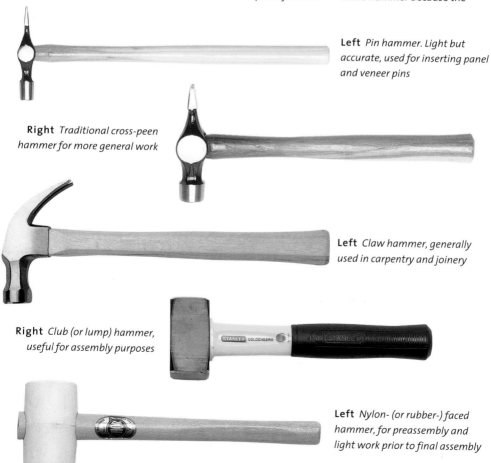

Left *Pin hammer. Light but accurate, used for inserting panel and veneer pins*

Right *Traditional cross-peen hammer for more general work*

Left *Claw hammer, generally used in carpentry and joinery*

Right *Club (or lump) hammer, useful for assembly purposes*

Left *Nylon- (or rubber-) faced hammer, for preassembly and light work prior to final assembly*

ringing sound of a steel hammer will change as the joint is knocked home, thereby giving skilled craftspeople greater control over their work.

Screwdrivers

It is important to use screwdrivers that exactly fit the slot in your screw heads. This can be achieved by taking a full set of screwdrivers and, if necessary,

grinding the ends of the blades to suit the heads of your screws. Screws have the benefit of actually pulling components together without the need for clamps. So, where it is difficult to apply a clamp to a curved component or where you do not have a clamp of the right size, consider fitting screws and covering the heads of the screws with wooden pellets.

Modern "cross-headed" screws have finely cut threads which have superior holding power in end grain lumber. Where it is necessary to hold components together using screws, which in some cases may be a better joint than conventional joinery, modern screws must be used. Crossheaded screwdrivers should be chosen carefully to fit the type and brand of screw being used.

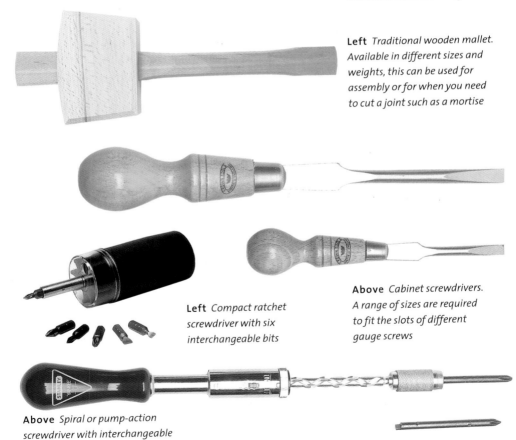

Left *Traditional wooden mallet. Available in different sizes and weights, this can be used for assembly or for when you need to cut a joint such as a mortise*

Left *Compact ratchet screwdriver with six interchangeable bits*

Above *Cabinet screwdrivers. A range of sizes are required to fit the slots of different gauge screws*

Above *Spiral or pump-action screwdriver with interchangeable bits that enable it to be used with any type of screw*

Band saws

OF ALL THE SMALL woodworking machines on the market, the band saw is perhaps one of the most versatile, as well as one of the most misused. Provided that the band is changed regularly – the smaller the band saw, the more frequently this needs to be done – and the band is kept properly tensioned and adjusted within its guides, then a small band saw is capable of accurate ripsawing, crosscutting and, unlike the table saw, doing curved work and deep ripsawing or resawing. If you let the band go dull and fail to keep it properly adjusted, you will fight to make the band saw maintain a cut near the line that you intended.

Tracking mechanism at rear of top band wheel

Band-saw band running around top and bottom wheels

The upper guide block mechanism can be raised or lowered according to the size of the job being cut

Rubber or cork surfaces on band wheels provide grip for the band

Guide locks to band both above and below the band-saw table

Table can be adjusted to tilt, thereby giving up to 45° angle cuts

Drive pulley from the motor

Brush rubbing against lower band wheel to remove dust from the surface of the wheel

Above *The band saw with its doors open, showing the two wheels on which the blade runs, the tensioning device adjustable*

for different-sized blades, the table with a straight fence and the sliding protractor head

Critical dimensions on a band saw include the height under the guides once they are raised – this is the theoretical limit of the thickness or width of the piece of wood the saw can cut. Most small band saws should really be restricted to cutting lumber of no thicker than about 4 to 6 inches. It is, however, possible to resaw boards of up to 10 inches, but this requires a more powerful band saw than is normally used in the home workshop. The second major critical dimension on the band saw is the throat. This is the distance from the blade to the pillar of the band saw. A throat of about 15 inches is usually perfectly adequate for most work in a small workshop.

The band

The essence of the band saw is the band itself. Bands are generally available in two blade types: normal and skip tooth. The latter is more suitable for working with dry hardwood. Bands also usually come in two types of steel: standard or bimetal. Bimetal means that the front section of the blade has been hardened by heating it to produce teeth with harder

Left *A band saw with its doors closed and ready for use. The table can be tilted, as here, to make angled cuts*

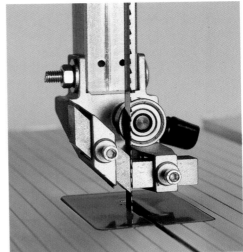

Above *A detail of the guide mechanism for the saw blade. The two blade guides are positioned either side of the blade to keep it running in lines; the thrust bearing behind the blade rotates so as to take up the pressure when sawing*

cutting edges and longer life. The rear section of the blade is not treated and so is in a softer, flexible condition. These blades are preferable to standard ones and can be resharpened by a competent saw sharpening service perhaps two or three times before being discarded. This is because it is not possible to reset the teeth of the blade, and, as the blade is resharpened, so the set is reduced and the kerf (width) of the cut is reduced.

The blade is placed on the band wheels and tensioned, and should run in roughly the middle of the width of the band wheel, which can be adjusted by turn-ing the tracking knob at the rear of the upper band wheel. Once the blade is tracking correctly, the blade guides should be set around the blade, both above and below the band-saw table. The blade guides are adjusted so that they give support to the blade but are no closer to the blade than the thickness of a piece of paper, and not actually touching or rubbing against the stationary blade.

Various widths of band-saw blade are available, depending upon the size of your machine. The narrower bands can be used for cutting tighter and tighter curved work.

Below *Different types of band-saw blade with varying numbers of teeth per inch (TPI)*

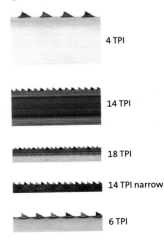

4 TPI

14 TPI

18 TPI

14 TPI narrow

6 TPI

16 TPI

Table saws and other power tools

THE TABLE SAW is one of the most useful machine tools for the furniture-maker's workshop. It enables lumber to be cut with accurate precision, either by ripping along the grain or by crosscutting (dimensioning) it to length. There are various different models of table saw on the market, available in a range of sizes and offering useful features.

Table saws

Table saws use modern tungsten carbide-tipped (TCT) circular saw blades to produce a cut almost as smooth as that produced by a plane. They are, therefore, frequently favored over band saws, which produce a slightly coarser cut. Table saws are popular small machines in cabinetmaking and joinery workshops, having the flexibility of ripping components to width as well as crosscutting or dimensioning components to length. A modern 10-inch table saw is capable of a depth of cut that enables it to do most of the work required in a small workshop. They can also be used for setting dadoes and cutting tapered components. One of the most endearing qualities of the table saw for the beginner, however, is the accuracy with which a line can be sawn straight and square.

Miscellaneous saws

A radial arm saw is a much more specialized piece of equipment, which is particularly good at crosscutting. Although there are other tasks that the radial arm

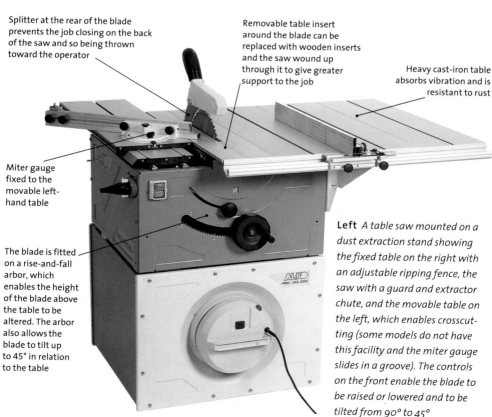

Splitter at the rear of the blade prevents the job closing on the back of the saw and so being thrown toward the operator

Removable table insert around the blade can be replaced with wooden inserts and the saw wound up through it to give greater support to the job

Heavy cast-iron table absorbs vibration and is resistant to rust

Miter gauge fixed to the movable left-hand table

The blade is fitted on a rise-and-fall arbor, which enables the height of the blade above the table to be altered. The arbor also allows the blade to tilt up to 45° in relation to the table

Left *A table saw mounted on a dust extraction stand showing the fixed table on the right with an adjustable ripping fence, the saw with a guard and extractor chute, and the movable table on the left, which enables crosscutting (some models do not have this facility and the miter gauge slides in a groove). The controls on the front enable the blade to be raised or lowered and to be tilted from 90° to 45°*

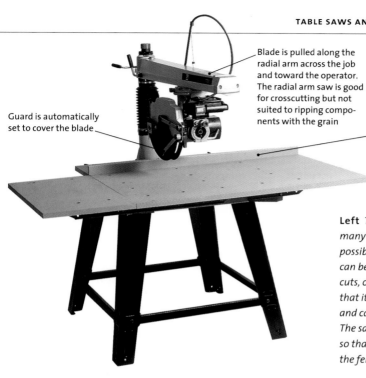

Blade is pulled along the radial arm across the job and toward the operator. The radial arm saw is good for crosscutting but not suited to ripping components with the grain

Guard is automatically set to cover the blade

Rear fence and table give support to the job for an accurate, clean cut as the saw's head tilts for 45°, compound and miter cuts

Left *The radial arm saw offers many different positioning possibilities for cutting. The saw can be canted to make angled cuts, or turned through 90° so that it is in line with the fence and can be used for ripping. The saw gantry can be angled so that angles other than 90° to the fence can be accomplished.*

saw can do, such as cutting moldings and miter joints and, in some cases, providing the platform for the addition of a router, by and large the radial arm saw is used only as a cross-cut saw. Since a saw of this type often needs a large supporting table either side of the saw, the space it occupies in a small workshop cannot be justified.

The miter, or snip-off, saw is a circular saw hinged to a table and fence, dedicated to cross-cutting or miter cutting relatively small components. Although a stationary machine, it is usually light enough to be carried to a location and used on-site.

A more common kind of site saw is the light, portable circular saw.

The final type of sawing machine common in small workshops is the scroll, or fret, saw. This is a motorized frame saw, usually with a very thin blade, which is useful for sawing thin, tightly curved components. Modern versions of this machine are now so accurate that the cuts produced are often slightly blackened, are smooth and clean and frequently need no other finishing work prior to assembly.

Above *A typical saw blade*

Above *The scroll, or fret, saw, which gives very fine cuts with fairly tight turns in shapes such as those found in jigsaw puzzles*

Planers and thicknessers

THE MACHINES USED for preparing lumber are called planers, planer/thicknessers, thicknessers or jointers. A planer or jointer is used for preparing the initial reference surface because, in the process of drying, lumber tends to cup and twist after it has been sawn into planks. To deal with this, these machines need to have a relatively long table either side of the cutter block in order to take out that twist or cup and leave a dead flat surface. Such machines need to produce not only a smooth planed surface but also a flat one. Planers have a relatively narrow cutter head in order to accommodate boards 8–12 inches (200–300 mm) wide. Since it is poor practice to plane lumber much wider than 10 inches – because of possible warping – it would be false economy to buy a planer with a cutter head much wider than this. There are narrower machines available, frequently called jointers. These have a cutter head of 6–8 inches and can be used for small components or for edge jointing wider boards.

The thicknesser

The thicknessing table, which is a machine table beneath the cutter head, is used to plane a surface parallel to your component's first or face side. The table itself is set at a predetermined distance from the underside of the cutter head. Planers frequently have thicknessing tables as part of their construction, and they can be converted into a thicknessing machine by having the planer tables lifted out of the way. Such a planer might well be called a planer/ thicknesser. Separate machines are also available just

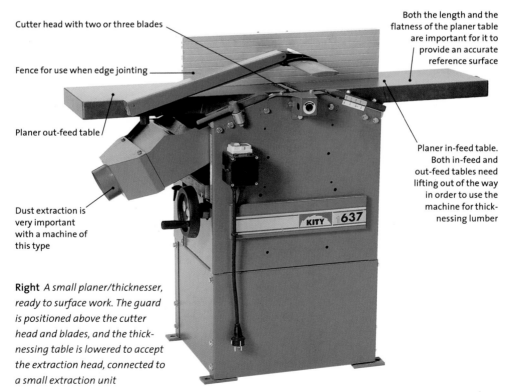

Cutter head with two or three blades

Fence for use when edge jointing

Planer out-feed table

Dust extraction is very important with a machine of this type

Both the length and the flatness of the planer table are important for it to provide an accurate reference surface

Planer in-feed table. Both in-feed and out-feed tables need lifting out of the way in order to use the machine for thicknessing lumber

KITY 1637

Right *A small planer/thicknesser, ready to surface work. The guard is positioned above the cutter head and blades, and the thicknessing table is lowered to accept the extraction head, connected to a small extraction unit*

Left *This jointer is a simple machine made primarily for surfacing narrow components, and has no built-in thicknessing capacity. The two hand wheels on the front adjust the in-feed and out-feed tables*

Above *Built solely to act as a thicknesser, this machine is used to plane the lumber to thickness using a flat surface as a reference*

Above *Hand-held electric planer*

for thicknessing lumber. (Rather confusingly, these machines are referred to as planers in some countries.) Planers have two or three cutter knives set in a head that revolves at high speed. The depth of cut of these knives is affected by the setting of the in-feed table on a planer and by the position of the thicknessing table on a thicknesser.

All of these machines, and most particularly the thicknesser, should be used in conjunction with a dust extractor, since they produce large quantities of shavings and wood dust. If not collected, the shavings are a fire risk and the dust is a health hazard. A further type of planer is a hand-held electric planer. Largely used as a site tool by joiners and carpenters, this has very little use in the workshop.

Leaving it to the experts

While every woodworker has to go through the process of preparing lumber for each and every job, you may decide that this initial lumber preparation, which after all is only a small part of the overall process of completing your project, could best be done by sub-contracting it to a local joinery firm. This would mean you would not need to install expensive machines that take up a considerable amount of space in your workshop and are used for only a very small proportion of the time.

Should you adopt this approach, you may find it useful to have a small jointer like the one pictured above, for use after your lumber has been prepared and for when you are working with much smaller components.

Right *Example of a stand which, using either a series of rollers (as here), is useful for supporting long stock as it comes off the saw or planer*

Routers

A ROUTER CONSISTS of a powerful motor, often fitted with a variable speed setting, which sits on top of two columns attached to a router base plate. The motor moves up and down on these columns against two springs. At the base of the motor is a collet, which accepts interchangeable cutters called router bits. The machine works by spinning the cutter at a very high speed, as high as 27,000 rpm. The cutter can be lowered into the job by pressing down on the motor against the springs in the two columns, or set at a predetermined position and then entered into the job sideways. Alternatively, the router can be set upside down in a small table with the cutter protruding above the table and the job fed across the table.

The fact that a router can accept so many differently shaped router bits gives this power tool exceptional versatility. It would probably be true to say that the invention of the plunged router has revolutionized woodworking, making it possible for even a relatively unskilled person to cut moldings, shape components, rout square and clean rabbets, plug mortises and do many other operations that would otherwise have required a whole bagful of hand tools. The modern router is in effect a small versatile mini-workshop that enables you to undertake a wide range of machining operations at no great cost.

The main choice available offers a small machine with a ¼-inch (6–mm) collet capable of taking a wide variety of smaller router bits, or a larger router, as shown below, with a ½-inch (13 mm) collet, capable of taking not only the small ¼-inch router bits but also the larger router bits with ½-inch shanks. Many woodworkers find the smaller router more comfortable and pleasant to use, being lighter and more manageable. There may well be occasions, however, when one cannot avoid using a cutter with a ½-inch shank.

Right *A hand-held heavy-duty router and guide rail, showing the arrangement of the fence and the collet that accepts the router cutters*

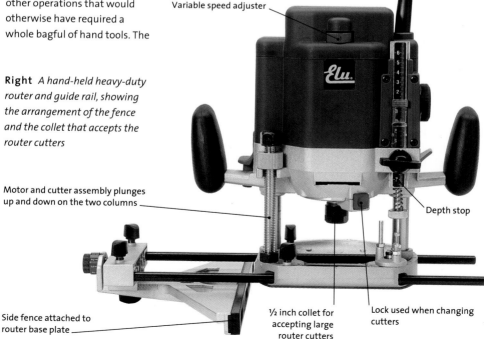

Variable speed adjuster

Motor and cutter assembly plunges up and down on the two columns

Depth stop

Side fence attached to router base plate

½ inch collet for accepting large router cutters

Lock used when changing cutters

Such router bits are used for producing large moldings, for example a raised and fielded panel for a door.

Noise and dust

A worthwhile feature on some routers is the variable speed setting. This enables the speed of the motor to be adjusted to suit the size of the cutter being used. Because routers are extremely noisy, emitting a high-pitched scream, it is considerably beneficial, even when using a relatively small router bit, to be able to turn the speed down without affecting the performance of the cutter.

Besides the noise of these machines, another disadvantage is the dust. The dust particles produced by routers, especially when milling man-made boards, are micron fine, and a short session with a router not attached to a dust extractor can cover both the workshop and the operator in a shower of fine, lung-clogging dust. Thankfully, modern routers are becoming better designed and enable the operator to fix a dust extractor outlet to the machine without greatly impairing the visibility of the cutter head or the depth of cut. When buying a router, it is strongly recommended that you consider this feature very carefully and always use a router with a dust extractor, even for short runs.

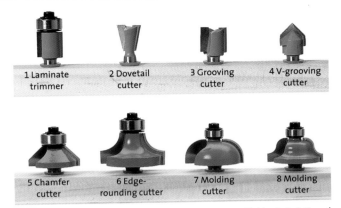

| 1 Laminate trimmer | 2 Dovetail cutter | 3 Grooving cutter | 4 V-grooving cutter |

| 5 Chamfer cutter | 6 Edge-rounding cutter | 7 Molding cutter | 8 Molding cutter |

Above *Examples of the range of router cutters available:* **1, 5, 6, 7** *and* **8** *have ball-bearing pilots fitted, which run along the edge of the work while the cutter makes the appropriate cut on the edge of the work;* **2, 3** *and* **4** *require guiding with a fence*

Router bits

It is the ability to change router bits quickly and without great expense that makes routers so versatile. Router bits are available in a wide variety of shapes and sizes. They basically fall into two categories: bits that are used for dimensioning lumber or cutting joints, such as straight bits or rabbet bits, and bits that are used for creating decorative moldings. Router bits are available in high-speed steel (HSS) or tungsten carbide-tipped (TCT). HSS bits are less expensive and can produce a finer, sharper cut, but they hold their edge for a relatively short time. TCT bits have the ability to hold their edge for longer but the edge is not quite so sharp as an HSS bit, and they are more expensive. TCT bits can be resharpened by a tool-sharpening service provided by your local tool shop. It is also possible to "touch up" a dull HSS bit using a small hand-held abrasive stone.

Right *Router connected to a small extractor*

Portable saws

MORE USEFUL ON SITE than in the workshop, portable saws are useful for a variety of tasks and can also be used mounted in a machine table as described below.

Right *A cordless version of a small, portable circular, or contractor's, saw*

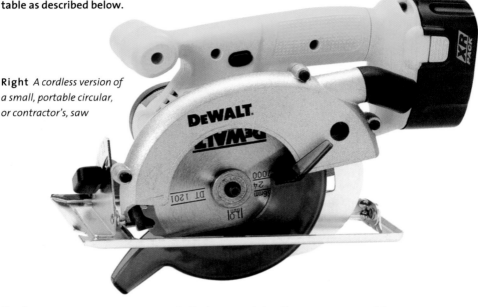

Circular saws

The circular saw, or contractor's saw, is the power tool highly favored for joinery site work. It can be taken to the job and used to trim components to length or to rip large sheets of man-made board into smaller component sizes. Two types are available. The more common one is where the blade is adjusted to cut a certain depth and is started up and run before the saw is engaged with the job. The second type is the plunge-cut saw. This, like the plunge router, can be lowered into the job and is especially useful for cutting out window openings in large sheets of man-made boards.

In the home workshop it is more common to find the circular saw turned upside down and positioned in a machine table. This can be either a home-made machine table made from a sheet of melamine-based MDF, or a purposely designed machine table that will accept several power tools, for example router, jigsaw and circular saw. By using a site saw in this way, you can have the benefits of a small stationary table saw without incurring high capital cost. A rip fence can be made from a piece of 2 x 2-inch (50 x 50–mm) lumber clamped to the table at either end, and a crosscut protractor can be bought as a

spare part from a saw manufacturer and then a dado groove routed across the surface of the machine table to accept it.

A new development in the circular saw market has been the cordless saw. This useful tool is small and light and can easily be used as a bench tool to trim or to dimension components.

Circular saw blades come in various blade patterns and tooth types. Tungsten carbide-tipped (TCT) blades are commonly available and are recommended for use on man-made boards, especially chipboard. Both rip and crosscut pattern blades are available for specialist applications, but generally most saws are fitted with combination blades that function relatively well in either situation.

Jigsaws

Jigsaws are hand-held power tools with a small reciprocating and narrow blade. Because of the narrowness of the blade, a jigsaw is most at home used for cutting curved components. Although new, stiffer blades, which are more accurate when used for ripping to a straight line, are available for some models, the jigsaw is not generally favored as a particularly accurate saw for dimensioning lumber. It could, however, be a useful saw for cutting up large sheet material into more easily handled sizes or large boards of lumber into small bulks. There is also a sanding system that enables the reciprocating action of the jigsaw to be used as a sanding tool. A similar type of saw is the multisaw. This is a tool that will hold a blade similar to, though more sturdy than, a jigsaw blade and will also hold a sanding system for freehand sanding.

Above *Small hand-held jigsaw*

Biscuit joiners

Biscuit joiners are one of the more useful power tools in the small furniture and shopfitting workshop. These are essentially tools that enable strong and quick joints to be made, using a flat "biscuit." The small saw creates a slot in both of the components being joined, into which the specially shaped biscuit fits. The strength of the joint is due to the close-fitting nature of the biscuit in the slot and the fact that the biscuit is made of compressed beech, which swells slightly on contact

Above *Glue dispenser and biscuits*

with the glue. Edge joints can very quickly be jointed together and accurately glued up with a biscuit jointer. The dispenser has been developed to put the right amount of glue quickly into each biscuit slot and saves time during the assembly process.

Right *A multisaw. The blade or sanding system operates in time with the tool*

Sanders

THE INVENTION of electrically powered sanding machines has certainly taken the backache out of the process of shaping and surface finishing.

Belt sanders

One of the most common electric sanders is the belt sander. Because a belt sander is so aggressively efficient at removing lumber, many people hesitate before using one for fine surface finishing. It is a relatively cumbersome machine and, as it moves around over the surface to be sanded, it is very possible to sand unevenly and create digs and gouges in an otherwise relatively smooth surface. This is because the sanding plate is relatively small. The plate on a 3-inch (75–mm) belt sander would probably be no larger than 3 inches square. Belt sanders are more useful for sanding narrow components like rails and stiles. Some belt sanders have a sanding frame that fits around the machine and effectively enlarges the area upon which the belt sander is sitting. This is a considerable improvement and is worthwhile if you are thinking of sanding a large area such as a tabletop

Basic hand-held belt sander

using a small belt sander. Small stands are available, too, which enable the belt sander to be turned upside down and converted into a small stationary sanding machine. This is another worthwhile accessory, and a stationary sanding machine is often more useful in the workshop than a portable power tool.

Random orbital sanders

For finishing large areas, the orbital sander was a popular power tool for many years. This sander has a flat rectangular pad that oscillates in small circles and is effective, but can leave small circular marks on the finished job. This has been greatly improved upon by the introduction of the random orbital sander. As the name suggests, random orbital sanders sand with a circular action, but without leaving the tell-tale sanding marks left by a conventional orbital sander. The random action produces a smooth, clean surface without any sanding marks. It is not, however, a flattening sander and should be used only on work that has already been made flat with either a hand plane or a machine. Random orbital sanders have Velcro adhesive

Orbital sander

Random orbital sander

Detail sander

or self-adhesive pads that make tensioning the sanding pads very quick and efficient. Where possible, always use dust extraction with sanding machines of this kind as the dust and abrasive particles created and left *in situ* can cause further scratches to the work and should be best ducted away to a dust extractor.

Other types of sander

The detail sander is another comparatively recent addition to the range of power tools. It

Left *Combined sanding machine with a small disc sander and a belt sander*

Disc sanders

A dedicated disc sander is useful. The disc should be relatively large, since it cuts by virtue of its weight rather than its speed. If a sanding disc is run too fast, the abrasive is more likely to burn the job rather than cut it. A disc sander is most effective for sanding end grain true and square, but it can also be used to shape and polish end grain to a very high luster. A good sanding machine has a rigid table, which ensures that the job remains square with the sanding wheel, but which can also be adjusted to sand compound angles and complex shapes.

features a D-shaped sanding pad that is capable of reaching into the corners of preassembled cabinets. Since it is good practice to presand and prefinish before assembly those parts of the job that cannot be reached after assembly, detail sanders have only a limited use in the home workshop but are useful for some jobs, such as detail sanding around carvings.

Sanding machines come in many forms but the most useful one in the small workshop is a combined belt and disc sander. A small machine of this type is invaluable for shaping components using a coarse paper, and for finishing small components. The disc sander can be used to round off corners and sand end grain true and

flush; the belt sander can be used for edge sanding against a fence or for surface sanding small components.

Whereas a disc sander is good for creating and finish sanding convex edges, a separate sanding machine is needed for sanding concave curves. To do this, you could set up a small drum sander in the drill press or, alternatively, consider a small bobbin sander. This is a machine designed specially for this purpose. It moves the sanding bobbin up and down slightly during the sanding process, which has the benefit of preventing the sanding block from becoming clogged and burnt, as can happen without this oscillation.

Small dedicated disc sander

Sanding attachments for a power drill: **1** *Contour sander* **2** *Rotary flap sander* **3** *Foam drum sander*

Drills and mortising machines

THE SIMPLEST METHOD of making a hole in a piece of wood is to use an old-fashioned hand-cranked brace and bit with a lip-and-spur drill bit. The main advantage of such drill bits is that the small locating screw (brad point) in the middle of the drill bit holds the drill in the lumber, making the process extremely controllable as you work.

Hand-held electric drills are really designed for use with metal but they can do a fairly good job in woodwork. The best bit to use with a power drill is the metal-cutting version of the lip-and-spur bit. This has a brad point at the center which locates the drill at the start of its cut and two wing points that scribe the circumference of the hole.

Cordless drills and screwdrivers

Cordless power drills were originally invented for on-site use, but are now very popular in the home workshop simply because of their convenience. The disadvantage of many cordless drills, however, is that they are often quite large and unwieldy because of the rather large and cumbersome battery. Besides drilling holes, cordless drills may be used to drive in screws, but care must be taken not to drive the head too deep below the surface. A better option is a cordless screwdriver. This is fitted with a clutch or torque facility, which has a number of different settings that can be set so that the screw is only ever driven flush with the surface. The cordless screwdriver will also function perfectly well as a conventional hand-held

drill, making it the more useful tool of the two.

Drill stands

The benefit of a drill stand is that you can set up the drill vertically so that it is always going to function at 90° to the job. Since most holes are drilled at 90°, drill stands or the machine equivalent, called a drill press or drilling machine, are very popular workshop tools. Drill presses come in two forms. One has a ½-inch (13–mm) or a

Above *Simple drill stand that will accept an electric drill*

Right *Hand-held cordless electric drill with rechargeable battery*

Left *Drill press for bench mounting. Larger versions can be floor standing*

Below *Dedicated mortising machine*

They enable a job to be clamped under a cutter and moved sideways, left or right, or forward or backward.

Although a drill press is an easy machine to learn how to use, always make sure that the drill guard is in place and that the cutter is free to move before the machine is switched on; take care to remove any loose clothing, ties, cuffs or necklaces.

Mortising machines

A drill press can be modified to function as a mortiser, but this is practical for only very modest use. Dedicated mortising machines are far more efficient and far easier to use (see page 68). Mortising is the practice of creating a square hole, which is done by setting up a tool called a mortising bit. Mortising bits have a drill, not unlike the lip-and-spur drill bit, which is matched to a square hollowed chisel. The lip-and-spur drill bit cuts slightly in front of the chisel, and the sharpened points of the hollowed chisel cut out the square corners around the drill bit. A mortising machine holds the mortise tool, enabling it to be driven down into the job, and holds the job in place while the tool is lifted out. The mortising machine also allows the job to travel sideways, left and right, thereby enabling the mortise tool to cut several square cuts side by side, thus creating a deep slot or mortise.

⅝-inch chuck guarded by a clear plastic guard. This works against a movable table that can be wound up or down a column using a small handle working on a rack and pinion. The other version is a floor-standing model, which allows you to drill longer objects. On the top of the drill press, inside a casing, is a series of pulleys that enable the position of the belt running on them to be changed, so as to change the speed of the drill. This is an extremely useful facility, allowing the drill to be slowed down when using large drill bits or sanding wheels. The depth of cut taken by the drill is controlled by a depth stop on the quill of the machine. This is the part of the machine that holds the drill chuck and moves up and down when the drill is driven into the job.

Drill presses are extremely versatile and can be used as sanding machines with the addition of flap wheels or small sanding drums (see page 37), as mortising machines with the addition of a mortising attachment or as milling machines with the addition of a cross vise.

Drill bits

Flat drill bits are very useful for drilling large holes; make sure that the point of the bit is engaged with the job before starting the drill. Lip-and-spur bits are those most widely used by woodworkers; they locate easily in the start position with a central brad point and do not deflect away from the job when the power is turned on.

Forstner bits are unlike most other types of boring bits in that they are guided by their rims and not by the center point or spiral. Holes bored with Forstner bits are clean and accurate, and flatter bottomed. Only Forstner bits can bore half a hole on the edge of a board or overlapping holes. They are completely unaffected by grain or knots in the lumber. Sawtooth bits, with saw teeth around the rim as well as a cutting edge, are better in end grain work.

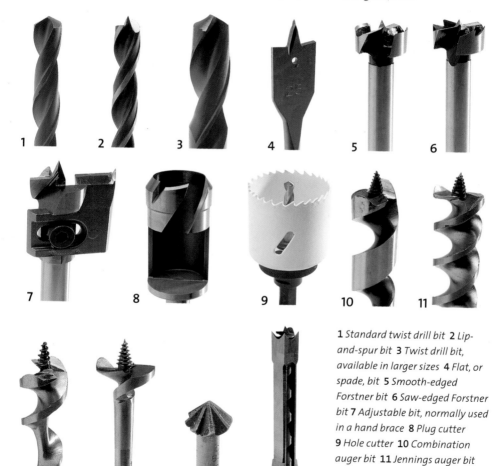

1 *Standard twist drill bit* 2 *Lip-and-spur bit* 3 *Twist drill bit, available in larger sizes* 4 *Flat, or spade, bit* 5 *Smooth-edged Forstner bit* 6 *Saw-edged Forstner bit* 7 *Adjustable bit, normally used in a hand brace* 8 *Plug cutter* 9 *Hole cutter* 10 *Combination auger bit* 11 *Jennings auger bit* 12 *Irwin auger bit* 13 *Ridgeway center bit* 14 *Countersink bit* 15 *Hollow mortising chisel with center auger*

Woodworking techniques

THIS SECTION COVERS the basic techniques required to prepare and work with lumber, using hand tools as well as small machines. The whole process is covered – from the initial start with an unplaned rough board of sawn lumber, progressing from preparing the lumber and sawing it into smaller components, to planing it on both sides and dimensioning it.

Beyond the key basic techniques for preparing and working with wood are the more advanced ones of routing, mortising, milling and shaping. All of them, once mastered, will eventually enable you to produce the essentials of woodworking – accurate joints and shaped components.

Lumber selection and cutting

LUMBER SELECTION is worth very careful thought for two reasons. First, you need to decide on the final effect that you want – where it will fit into the home, the color and grain pattern that will be most suitable and any other consideration that will affect lumber choice.

Second, see what is available at your lumber supplier so that you can buy boards that will allow you to cut your components economically and use lumber of suitable stability.

The cutting list

The start of a project is always exciting. Always remember, however, that you can save yourself a great deal of time and money by first planning what you are going to do before you buy your lumber. First, make up a list of all of the components required for your project and put against each component its dimensions – length, width and thickness. This list is called a cutting list and is used to help you in the purchase and selection of your lumber. Try, for example, to design your components so that they can easily be planed from 1-inch (25-mm) or 2-inch (50-mm) rough boards. It is common practice for lumberyards to saw lumber to 1¼ inches (30 mm), which dries down and shrinks to slightly over 1 inch. A board of this thickness will give you a planed component of roughly ¾ inch (20 mm) when planed on both sides. A 2-inch board will give you a finished component thickness of approximately 1¾ inches (45 mm).

Consider whether you need particularly stable components such as drawer sides or the loose leaf on a drop-leaf table. In both these instances you would want to use quarter-sawn lumber, which is particularly stable and less likely to cup or warp. Consider also whether you are buying kiln-dried or air-dried lumber. With the latter you must allow a period of at least one to two weeks after your initial planing of the lumber for the wood to settle and acclimatize to your workshop's humidity. If you are using kiln-dried lumber you can expect the lumber to warp or twist much more quickly but for much shorter periods. In this case, the planing or machining of the lumber is releasing stresses within the lumber that were placed there in the drying process.

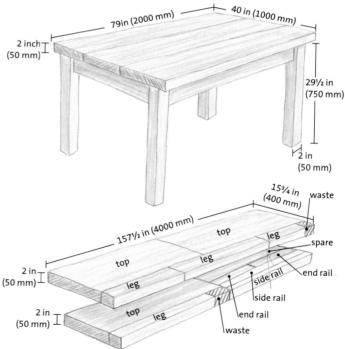

Above *The visual cutting list (above) shows one possible way of cutting the lumber for this table (top) from two planks, i.e., four legs, two long side rails, two shorter end rails and a top made of three pieces*

Marking and cutting the lumber

Once you have selected your lumber and brought it to the workshop, select which board will give you which component. Stand the boards on end so that they are easier to turn over. The first crosscut is critical, for, although it makes the boards much easier to handle once they are shorter, the options for using that board for long components are then reduced.

Use a chalk line to mark lines down the length of the board as illustrated below. At this stage do not attempt to come near to your finished sizes – just cut the components ³⁄₁₆ inch (5 mm) or so oversize.

Having marked chalk lines down the length of your rough-sawn board it is time to saw down the lines. This process is best done on a band saw. Here the band saw would be used freehand without any fence or guides, and you simply need to guide the saw down the chalk line. A steady hand and good lighting around the band saw table help accomplish this task. Make sure that your band saw is fitted with a sharp blade and is properly tensioned. Also check that the movable blade guides are set so that no more than ³⁄₈ inch (10 mm) of blade is exposed above the lumber. Keep your hands well back from the blade and do not let this machine lull you into a false sense of security. Although the band saw is a relatively gentle machine to use, it is still capable of inflicting a very painful and damaging cut to precious fingers.

PREPARATION AND MARKING

1 First brush the boards you have selected with a wire brush to remove all dirt, grit and foreign material, which could blunt your tools.

2 Use a chalk line to mark lines down the length of the board. This is a tool frequently used in the construction industry.

3 The line is drawn out of the container through the chalk and is snapped on to the job, leaving a straight, clean, colored line on the wood.

THE JIGSAW

4 If you do not have a band saw the hand-held power jigsaw is a good alternative tool for sawing wood both with and across the grain.

The first step in preparing lumber

ONCE YOUR BOARDS have been sawn into smaller components, the next step is to plane them on one side. This could be done by hand, but most woodworkers either use a planer or sub-contract this job to a small joinery shop. The surface planer is a relatively simple machine and, properly guarded, can be very safe to use. The problem is that the main guard is easily removable and, once removed, this machine is potentially very dangerous. If you have not already done so (see page 43), run a wire brush over the surface of the board before using the planer. This removes any grit that could easily damage the cutter head or table.

Using the planer

Before starting, set the in-feed table ³⁄₆₄ inch (1 mm) lower than the height of the blades. Now set the position of the guard. This extends the full width of the cutter blades. To be especially careful, move the back vertical fence forward so that only the width of your components plus about ³⁄₈ inch (10 mm) is showing in front of the vertical fence. The guard will now cover any protruding blade right up to that rear fence. The height of the fence should now be adjusted so that you can just pass your lumber beneath it.

To use the planer, start the motor; then lay your component on the in-feed table – usually the right-hand table. Now push the job over the cutters; you should hear a change of tone as the cutters engage the job. As the job appears on the out-feed table, transfer your weight so that the palm of your left hand is pressing the front of the job on to the out-feed table. As the job passes further over the cutters, transfer your weight from the in-feed table to the out-feed table. As you do this, lift your other hand over the guard, but do not at any time place your hands or fingers anywhere near the cutter guard. Always remember, when using any machine involving a revolving cutter head, that any loose clothing and long hair should be out of the way. Any jewelry should be removed and you should check the floor for any slippery surfaces or trailing leads.

Creating a reference surface

As you pass the lumber over the cutter, you will gain a clearer idea of whether the board has cupped or is in any way twisted by seeing which areas of the board have not touched the cutter blocks.

It is essential to create a flat reference surface, or face side, using the planer. From this reference surface all the other

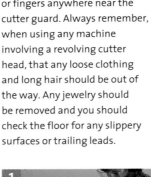

USING THE PLANER

1 Wearing safety goggles and ear protection, lay the component on the in-feed table. Start pushing it over the cutters.

2 Lift your left hand carefully over the cutter guard.

3 Start to transfer pressure to the out-feed table.

4 Transfer all your weight to the out-feed table as the job progresses.

5 With pressure now on the out-feed table only, finish the cut.

SUBSEQUENT STAGES
6 Inspect the first pass to determine if any subsequent operations are needed.

sides of your component will be made: the edges at 90° to the face side; the opposite side parallel to the face side; the ends at 90° to the face side. So this surface is worth planing carefully and marking with a small "F." Traditionally, the F leans into the direction in which the grain runs and the stem of the F also points toward the face edge (see page 46).

You may get tear-out—small or rough patches—where the grain has been torn out when you pass your component across the planer. If this occurs, turn the board round and try planing in the other direction. This is called planing with the grain.

Using the thicknesser

Once the face side has been planed, the opposite side can be done. The face side can be used on the machine table of your thicknesser as the reference surface. This thicknessing table is moved up and down beneath your cutter block and positioned to plane a surface parallel to the face side and at a given distance from that side. You will need ear protection when using the planer and especially the thicknesser. Also, the thicknesser is capable of producing a high volume of chippings and dust, so it is essential to fit a dust extractor to the machine.

A thicknessing machine drives the component underneath the cutters. Since you do not have to push the lumber there is a slight danger that your fingers can be trapped against the side of the thicknesser or the support rollers. Never bend down to see whether a thicknesser is clogged up and never put your hand on the thicknessing table to move a scrap of wood or pull out a jammed component.

Aim at this stage to thickness your components $\frac{1}{16}$ inch (2 mm) oversize. Then leave them stacked overnight, resting on small sticks that allow air to reach all four sides of the newly planed boards.

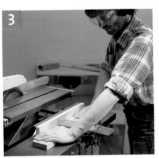

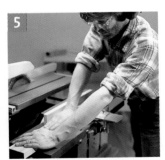

7 Next, guide the lumber through the thicknesser.

8 Check the thickness of the lumber with calipers.

Machining edges and cutting to width

PLANING A FACE edge means creating a straight side at right angles to the component's face, or reference, side. The F or face marks point in the direction of the side to be used as a face edge, which has already been ripped roughly straight with the band saw. Before setting the face side against the planer's vertical fence, first move the fence toward the front edge of the planer tables to reduce to a minimum the amount of exposed blade. Check the vertical fence against the in-feed table for square, using a good light source and engineer's square, and position the guard, allowing just enough room between the vertical fence and the guard for the job to pass over the cutter blocks. When planing an edge, try to plane with the grain.

After having planed one face edge, use a table saw or a band saw to cut a line parallel to the face edge at a predetermined distance from it. If your finished components should be 4 inches (100 mm), you should saw your components to 4 1/16 inches (101–102 mm), allowing a further 1/16 inch (1–2 mm) to be planed off to final dimension. This is called sawing and planing to final dimension and enables you to get the components to the exact size for your project.

Ripping with a table saw

When ripping with a table saw – probably the most accurate way of creating a sawn straight edge – you need to use the rip fence. This is a fence set parallel to the saw blade and movable to a preset distance from the blade.

The distance the rip fence is set from the saw blade will be the size of the component when it emerges. There are several important things to remember when ripping. First, there is the splitter and guard. A splitter is a steel plate at the rear of the table saw blade. Usually, the guard is attached to the top of the splitter and from there covers the crown of the saw blade. Both the guard and the splitter perform essential functions and neither should ever be removed when you are

USING A PLANER

1 Set up the planer ready to make the first pass for planing a component's face edge.

2 Set the face side of the component against the vertical fence and leave the minimum amount of blade exposed.

sawing. The function of the splitter is to prevent boards, particularly kiln-dried ones, that are being ripped from closing on the saw blade after they have been cut. This can occur when lumber has been dried very quickly and contains tensions that are released in the sawing process. If this happens and the splitter is not in position, there is a considerable risk that the lumber could be thrown back at the machinist. Set the saw blade square, checking it with an engineer's square against the surface of the table saw. Set the guard to a height so that there is a gap between the component and the bottom of the guard of no more than ⅜ inch (10 mm). With the guard and the rip fence

in place, rip the components to dimension. Keeping your fingers well away from the saw blade, press in toward the rip fence and forward to push the component through the saw. As the component is sawn, so your hands approach the spinning blade. Do not go too near – use a preprepared push stick rather than put your fingers near the saw. Never pull lumber through a table saw from the rear. When ripping, occasionally a very thin strip of waste lumber is produced to the side of the saw blade, which can be thrown back at you. Always wear a face mask and ear protection when ripping.

Note: for reasons of clarity, the illustrations below show the guard in position, but without

the dust extraction pipe fitted to it.

Ripping with a band saw
A band saw can also be used for ripping. Set up the blade so that it is cutting at true right angles to the band-saw table. Set the blade guides so that they are approximately ⅜ inch (10 mm) above the component, with the blade guard above that, and set the rip fence the required distance from the blade. A band saw will give a slightly coarser cut than a table saw, but, provided the blades are changed regularly, a band saw can produce very accurate work and is a useful machine in a small workshop.

USING A TABLE SAW
3 Press the component in toward the fence and forward.

4 Always use push sticks rather than fingers for safety's sake.

5 Take care that the thin strip of waste lumber that is produced does not get thrown up at you.

USING A BAND SAW
6 A band saw is another useful machine that can be used for ripping components.

Marking out for accuracy

"MARKING OUT" is the process of marking on components the exact dimensions – either of the components themselves or of some aspects of the joinery on that particular component. If some components are identical, simply use one test piece component to set up your machines to cut the entire batch to the same size.

Good marking out is vitally important for the accuracy of subsequent work. Take your time to get it absolutely right and then relax in the knowledge that you have set secure foundations for your project. If you mark out accurately and then cut to the line, the component cannot help but fit.

Using marking knives

Very little marking out in a cabinetmaking workshop is done with a pencil, because a pencil line has a thickness, no matter how sharp the pencil may be. A marking knife, however, provides a mark of absolute accuracy. This is because a marking knife is sharpened with one bevel so that when it is used and a line is struck with the knife held at 90° to the job, it provides a cut into the job that denotes the exact end of your component. A line struck accurately with a marking knife will remain on the job after the joint is cut, after it is assembled and when the job is finished. The bevel side of your marking knife should always face the waste side of your component or joint.

When using a square with a marking knife, hold the square tight against the job, with your fingers pulling the start of the square into the job. Place your knife on the mark that denotes the dimension of your component and then slide the square up to your knife. Now grip the square tightly in position and strike a line by drawing your marking knife down the outside of the blade of your square. Squares should be of extremely high-quality steel since marking knives can quickly wear down a blade of inferior quality.

Using rules and squares

There is a technique for using rules with absolute accuracy. Should you require, for example, a component 23¼ inches (591 mm) long, place the rule with the 23¼-inch dimension mark in line with the end of your component. Sight this very carefully by looking down on the line. Avoid any errors of parallal marking by looking at this from left or right and adjust the rule so that it is lying on your component and overhanging the end of it by exactly the right amount. Now strike a small line with your marking knife, using the end of the rule as the reference point. This is much more accurate than aligning the rule's zero with the end of the component and attempting to tick a line at the required measurement.

When using a square to check for squareness, place the stock of the square against the face of your job and slide it down so that the blade is just touching the edge. Slide along the edge of the job with a good strong light source at the back of the blade, so you can check for squareness.

Using gauges

A marking gauge is a simple tool, primarily used to scribe a line along the grain of the wood. The point of the marking gauge can be filed and adjusted so that it cuts a neat and clear line. It should be sharpened in a similar way to a marking knife, and used so that the beveled side of the blade is always on the waste side of your cut. Either draw a marking gauge toward you or push it away. When setting a gauge, set it by tapping the stop of the gauge against your bench. Once set, slightly tighten the adjusting screw.

A cutting gauge is set in exactly the same way and is a very similar tool, but it has a small knife rather than a steel point to make the mark on the job. Cutting gauges are most useful for marking across the grain of the lumber, although a properly sharpened ordinary marking gauge will do just as good a job as a cutting gauge.

ACCURATE MARKING AND MEASURING

1 Using a marking knife allows absolute precision. Grip the square tightly so you can mark against it.

2 Using the end of the rule as the reference point is an accurate measuring technique.

USING SQUARES

3 A good light source is essential for checking an edge for square, and the flatness of a piece.

DIFFERENT TYPES OF GAUGE

4 Using a marking gauge along the grain.

5 A cutting gauge is useful for cutting across the grain.

6 Calipers measure lumber thickness very precisely.

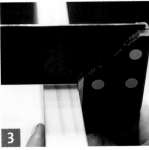

Using handsaws accurately

TO BE ABLE TO USE a handsaw with confidence and with accuracy is one of the great pleasures of woodworking. Many beginners find this such a frustrating mystery, however, that it drives them to pick up the nearest power tool or needlessly invest a great deal of money in machines that they feel will do the job more accurately than they ever could by hand. These pages describe, first, how to choose a saw for a particular job; second, how to support the job so that you can concentrate on sawing rather than holding the work; and, finally, how to control a saw and adjust your stance during the sawing process. It should be stressed, however, that using a handsaw is not difficult – the technique simply requires practice.

Choosing your saw

Choose your saw with care. Most sawing can be accomplished using either a small panel saw with a relatively short blade but with fine teeth, or a backsaw such as the tenon saw. Finer work should be done using a dovetail saw. Most cabinet-makers favor using a dovetail saw over a tenon saw and will set up a 10-inch dovetail saw with a relatively wide kerf to accomplish the jobs normally done by the slightly coarser and heavier tenon saw.

Holding the piece to be sawn

The most satisfactory way to hold the piece is by using a vise in a large, heavy bench. If you can use your bench in this way then you can set up your body to control the saw accurately and swing your arm in the correct manner. If, however, you also have to hold down a piece of wood that is jumping all over the place, you will probably not be standing in the right place to swing the saw accurately.

It is possible to saw board material when it is supported horizontally on sawhorses. Because the board material itself has sufficient weight to give it stability you will have less of a problem holding the job down while sawing.

Problems arise when you try to crosscut relatively small

HOLDING THE WORK SECURELY

1 Sawing down a line, with the work held vertically in the vise.

2 Sawing down the length of weighty board material supported on sawhorses. It is often helpful to extend your forefinger along the side of the saw handle as a guide, and to give you greater control as you saw.

3 It is hard to hold the job firmly when crosscutting a small piece of wood on a sawhorse or portable workbench.

pieces of wood while holding them down on a low sawhorse. In the example shown below, the craftsman is attempting to do two jobs at once – both saw the wood and hold it in position – and the chances of success are compromised.

A useful piece of equipment when sawing is a bench hook. This hooks over the edge of the workbench and allows you to secure the job in place without compromising the sawing stance. It is important that jobs much longer than the width of the bench hook are supported at their far end so that the job sits squarely on the bench hook, parallel to the bench surface.

If, before sawing begins, the scribed line is reinforced and cut quite deeply into the job, and a small fillet of waste wood is pared out to create a small channel, this enables the saw to make a clean start in the lumber. It also creates a clean scribed shoulder to the cut where the risk is that the saw would tear or fail to cut the fibers cleanly. This is especially useful in soft grained or fibrous wood.

Lighting

Always use a well-positioned bench light to illuminate the saw – if you cannot see where you are going, the chances of your cutting accurately to a line are infinitesimally small. A bench light can throw an invisible scribe line into high relief by catching it at the right angle. If you can see your scribe line, the chances are you can saw to it much more accurately.

Using the kerf

The kerf of the saw is the width of the cut created by the saw. The kerf is created by the teeth being bent to left and right to make a cut that is wider than the thickness of the saw plate. It is necessary to have a kerf that is wider than the plate of the saw so that you can guide the saw slightly left or right as you progress down a cut. However, if your saw cuts a very wide kerf, then it is going to require a great deal more energy and effort to make the cuts. Always try to reduce the kerf that saws make, since the less effort that you put into the cut, the more control you will have over the direction of the saw.

The aim is to saw with the kerf

Enlarged marking knife cut to support the first saw cut

4 A hardwood bench hook is useful for holding the wood when crosscutting small pieces. You can buy a ready-made one or make one yourself in the workshop.

5 Clearly scribe the cutting line before sawing. Then pare a "V" along this line with a chisel, which creates a small channel in which to rest the saw for the first cut.

in the waste side of the job. A good sawyer will do this: taking out one half of the scribed line and leaving just a faint trace of the scribed line still present on the job.

Learning how to saw

In order to understand how to use a saw properly, the process of ripsawing down a line has been broken down here into easily managed steps.

The first step is to mark out the job and set it up in your bench vise. In the illustrations opposite, a dovetail saw is being used to ripsaw a piece of fine-grained mahogany, about ¾ inch (20 mm) thick, which is being sawn down to a scribed crosscut line, probably 1⅜ inches (35 mm) from the end of the job. This is the kind of cut made when sawing dovetails or when ripping boards to width. Once the component is marked out, support it vertically in the end vise of a cabinetmaker's bench with no more than about 2 inches (50 mm) of the job protruding above the surface of the bench. Align the job with the end of the bench to make sure that the piece is upright. With the job held vertically, your ability to saw accurately down that line is greatly enhanced.

POSITIONING YOUR BODY Next, take up position with your legs 2 feet (600 mm) apart and your chest at right angles to the face

of the job. Take the saw in your hand and imagine a line drawn straight from the tip of your saw, through your hand, up your arm, past your elbow to your shoulder – this should form a perfectly straight line. The forward and backward action of the saw is a motion taken from the pivot of your shoulder, and that shoulder should be placed exactly in line with where you want to cut. Your chest should not be turned to face the job. Keep your body positioned sideways on as if you were about to serve a tennis ball. If you face the cut directly, the chances are that this body line will be compromised.

THE SAWING TECHNIQUE Now start the cut. Position a finger- or thumbnail in the gauge line to give the saw a starting location; then rest the saw against this finger- or thumbnail. The start is critical. Rest the tip of the saw lightly on the job and, with confidence, simply give one clean push.

Having made a clean start, now concentrate upon the direction in which the saw is going. The first two strokes of the saw will determine which way the saw is going to go. After two or three strokes, there is no point in attempting to correct the direction, so determining the saw's direction early on in its travel down the job is very important. Concentrate on the gauge line and "think" the saw

down this line.

At this stage it is essential to slacken your grip on the handle of the saw. A backsaw has a brass strip running down the back of the saw blade, which provides all the weight that is necessary to drive the saw into the job. If you grip the saw too hard you will increase the work that the teeth are being asked to do and drive the saw offline. So hold the saw like a child's hand. Increase your concentration. Do not attempt to control the direction of the saw by wiggling it left and right. Instead "think" the saw down the line. It is a little like riding a motorcycle down a winding country lane: you do not positively lean a bike over to take a fast corner, instead it is all to do with minute shifts of your body and concentration.

Move the bench light if necessary to enable you to see the line as you saw down it. Also make sure that you use the full length of the saw blade with fluid strokes of the saw. Next, concentrate on the stop – the specific point you are sawing down to – which is achieved by stopping sawing exactly on the marked line.

With a little practice it is possible to learn how to saw accurately with the kerf in the waste side of the cut with very little effort. The technique is not difficult to acquire and is extremely satisfying.

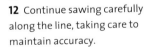

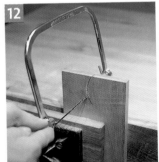

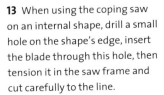

THE SAWING STANCE

6 The action of the saw forward and backward is a motion taken from the pivot of your shoulder, which should be placed exactly in line with the intended cut.

SAWING TECHNIQUES

7 The start is critical; use a fingernail in the gauge line to position the saw accurately.

8 Check the direction of the saw and ensure that the first few cuts follow the gauge line, sawing with the kerf in the waste side of the cut.

9 Relax your grip slightly on the handle so as not to drive the saw offline.

10 Saw with an easy action, "thinking" the saw down the line.

USING A COPING SAW

11 Use a coping saw to follow a curved line from the end of a job, starting with initial strokes.

12 Continue sawing carefully along the line, taking care to maintain accuracy.

13 When using the coping saw on an internal shape, drill a small hole on the shape's edge, insert the blade through this hole, then tension it in the saw frame and cut carefully to the line.

Using chisels

WHEN USING A CHISEL, the sharpness of the edge of this tool is of paramount importance. Never let the edge of your chisel become blunt. As soon as you feel that you need to exert undue pressure to make a paring, hone the edge of your chisel. When using a chisel consistently it is not unusual to need to hone an edge once every half hour or so.

Paring vertically

POSITIONING YOUR BODY To pare vertically, hold the chisel close to your body with your elbows tucked in so that you can exert the power of your shoulders and trunk rather than your hands and forearms. Rest your lower forearm on the job that you are paring, grip the blade of the chisel and exert an upward pressure. Your upper hand holds the handle of the chisel and exerts a downward pressure. In this way the chisel is held in tension, giving the user great power and control. You can drive it through end grain and yet control the cut, preventing the chisel from skating away from you and digging into the surface of the bench. (Note that it is best to use a cutting board to protect the surface of your bench.)

CHISEL WIDTH With a narrow chisel of ¼ inch (6 mm) it is possible to make a paring cut in a relatively soft wood, such as mahogany or walnut, that is the full width of the chisel. With a wider chisel than this it would be impossible to make a full-width paring cut and still retain control of the chisel. (In this instance you might want to use a mallet, but again control

HOLDING THE CHISEL FOR VERTICAL PARING
1 The lower hand rests on the job, the fingers gripping the blade of the chisel and pushing up. The upper hand grips the handle and pushes down.

would be lost.) Instead, wider chisels are used with their corners only to extend and enlarge the existing cut created by a narrow chisel taking a full width shaving. So a ¼-inch (6-mm) cut carefully pared at right angles across the end of the job would be enlarged using an ⁵⁄₁₆-inch (8-mm) chisel, taking a ¹⁄₁₆-inch (2-mm) paring to the

PARING END GRAIN WITH CHISELS OF DIFFERENT WIDTH
2 Take a narrow chisel and start paring, using the full width of the chisel.

left and to the right. The central ¼-inch cut would be untouched. The principle is to extend a cut using the widest chisel available because the width of the chisel will give you greater accuracy and flatness.

PARING BACK TO GAUGE LINES To pare back to a gauge line, never pare away a shaving that

3 Switch to a slightly larger size of chisel.

4 Enlarge the paring using the corners of the larger chisel.

PARING BACK TO A GAUGE LINE
5 Remove a thin shaving, taking it three-quarters of the way down the piece.

6 Turn the piece over and repeat the process from the other side.

7 Turn the piece over once more, back to its original position.

8 Repeat the process to produce a surface pared exactly at right angles to the face of the piece.

9 Here, the recess on the left has been pared correctly in stages, with thin shavings being removed, little by little. The right-hand recess is an example of paring attempted in one go. This produces a shaving that is too thick and uncontrollable and leads to inaccuracy.

is too thick. A chisel is really only a sharpened steel wedge; if the shaving you try to remove is too thick, then instead of allowing the chisel to make a paring at right angles to the surface it will drive the chisel back, possibly past your gauge line.

As you pare , approaching your gauge line, pare three-quarters of the way down the end grain, then turn the job over and pare three-quarters of the way down from the opposite side. In this way you will approach your gauge lines with the end grain of the board becoming more and more like a flat surface at right angles to the face side. As you approach the gauge lines, you are left with the final shaving. Click the chisel into the gauge line – you should be able to feel the sharp edge of the chisel engage in the gauge line – and you can then make the final cut three-quarters of the way down. Turn the job over and do exactly the same on the opposite side; pare three-quarters of the way down and you will be left with a true surface, hand pared at 90° to the face side.

Paring horizontally

There may well be occasions when you want to pare a job horizontally. In this case, clamp the job in the end vise of your bench, so that it is 6–8 inches (150–200 mm) above the surface of the bench. At this height the job will not vibrate too much, and it will allow you to get into the correct stance.

POSITIONING YOUR BODY Stand with your legs wide apart and your chest and shoulders at right angles to the job. A straight line should be formed from the blade of your chisel, through your wrist, up through your forearm to your elbow. This should be as near to parallel with the surface of your bench as possible. To achieve this, it may be necessary for you to spread your feet further apart, thereby lowering your elbow

and shoulder. In this stance, power is given to the cut by tucking your elbow tight into your chest and, once again, leaning on your knees and trunk rather than applying power with the arm and shoulder.

PARING CHISELS Greater control and flexibility can be achieved by using a paring chisel for paring horizontally. By using a long-bladed or long-handled chisel, the length of the tool enables you to exert much finer control over the cuts. Never use a paring chisel with a mallet. This is a delicate tool and should be kept for paring alone.

A cranked paring chisel has most use in a cabinetmaking workshop for cleaning out the inside of carcasses after assembly. Invariably, there will be a small amount of "squeeze-out" of glue on the inside of a

joint. If a cabinet has been waxed inside before being assembled then this glue will be easily removed by the careful application of the corner of the chisel. A long cranked paring chisel enables you to pare across the depth of even a fairly wide carcass.

Other uses for chisels

There may be times when you want to use a chisel with a mallet or a soft-faced hammer. Although this technique allows you to remove waste relatively quickly, you will pay for this with the inevitable loss of control since it is difficult to ensure that the chisel is held at right angles to the surface of the job.

One example where this is not necessary is when using a mortise chisel. Although mortises are almost always cut either with a drill press or a router, they can be cut by hand using a mortise chisel and a mallet. To do this, support the job above one bench leg, hold the mortise chisel with a straight arm and use a flat-faced wooden joiner's mallet, again with a straight arm. This straight-arm stance, as you stand at the end of the bench and face down the length of the job, enables the chisel to be drawn back along the length of the mortise, levering out the waste and at the same time siting the chisel and ensuring it is kept at 90° to the job.

Tenting

An alternative technique to paring down to a gauge line is called "tenting." This involves paring back to the gauge line as described earlier, but without attempting to work always at right angles to the face side. Instead, a tented surface is deliberately left between the two gauge lines. Then, when the gauge line on both sides of this ridged central area has been reached, this ridged area or "tent" is removed with a series of parallel shavings that gradually increase in length until they extend almost from one gauge line to the other.

"Tented" surface pared away from both sides

HOLDING THE CHISEL FOR HORIZONTAL PARING

10 Assume the correct stance for paring horizontally. A paring chisel is best used here since its length allows greater control.

USING A MORTISE CHISEL

11 A mortise chisel needs to be kept at 90° to the job. Cutting a mortise is best done over a bench leg, which provides extra support for the task.

12 A side view of the correct stance for holding a mortise chisel and mallet, ensuring that the work is firmly secured to the bench.

USING A CRANKED-NECK PARING CHISEL

13 Pare away surplus glue around a joint using a cranked-neck paring chisel.

ONCE YOUR HAND PLANE has been set up to work correctly it can be tested on a board. A correctly set up plane will have a slightly curved plane iron. The purpose of this is to create a shaving of approximately ⅝ inch (16 mm) in width. This is a narrow ribbon-like shaving, which emerges from the middle of the throat of the plane and is easily controllable.

A wider shaving than this can be created by using a flatter, less curved plane iron, but it would require much more energy to work and would give the operator much less control. The curved iron also creates a shaving with a thickness in its center of approximately 1/100 inch (0.25 mm), but this tapers out to nothing at the edges of the shaving.

Quite often, a hand plane is used to remove the machine marks left by a planer. You therefore need to plane over the surface evenly and with great control. If you make three parallel chalk marks across the job before you start, you will be able to see where the plane takes a shaving and what part of the board still needs to be planed. Once all the chalk marks have been removed, all the machine or planer marks will also have been removed. If further work is needed, the process can be repeated.

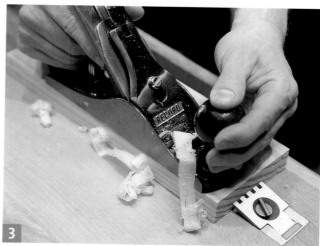

Planing with the grain
Always try to plane a board in the direction it wishes to be planed, i.e., *with* the grain. You can get some idea of which way the grain is running by looking at the edge of the board.

Correct use of the hand plane
When using a plane, you should be pressing down on the job, as well as moving the plane forward; therefore, the trunk of your body can exert considerable power downward if, and only if, the plane is kept close to your body. Begin planing with one

USING CHALK AS A GUIDE
1 Chalking across the job before starting enables you to see where the plane takes a shaving.

2 As the plane progresses, it becomes evident which part of the board still needs to be planed.

3 As you start the cut, the pressure is on the front of the plane, but as the cut progresses pressure should move so that it is on the rear handle in the final stage of the pass.

hand applying pressure on the front, or toe, of the plane. Move forward over the job by keeping your front foot forward and swaying over the work on your knees, rather than pushing the plane forward using only your forearms and shoulders. Transfer the pressure slightly as you move the plane forward and finish up with the other hand pressing down on the back, or heel, of the plane. Thus, a plane shaving can be started, stopped

and continued down a long board because the plane is kept close to the body and under control. Such control is not possible if the plane is extended too far forward. In a similar way a long board can be easily planed in a series of short steps, each time starting and stopping the plane under control.

Planing edges

Bear in mind that a plane iron is slightly curved. If the edge to be

planed is already square at right angles to the face edge and all you wish to do is take off a single shaving, then plane with the job in the middle of the sole of your plane. If you wish to correct the angle, then skew the plane off to one side or the other.

A shooting board (see page 61) is often used to plane the edges of thin board – less than ³⁄₈ inch (10 mm) thick – upon which it would be too difficult to balance a bench plane.

DETERMINING THE GRAIN

4 You can tell which way the grain is running by looking at the edge of the board.

HAND PLANING EDGES

5 You can remove a fine shaving to one side with a well-sharpened and adjusted plane.

6 Planing with the job in the middle of the plane's sole.

7 Positioning the plane off to one side of the job.

Hand planing across end grain

QUITE OFTEN, a sawn surface needs to be planed back to exact dimension along the grain, using a bench plane as previously described, or across the grain, using either the bench plane or a small block plane. If you are using a bench plane, you need to set up your job in the vise of your bench with the end grain facing up. Larger components such as carcass sides can be treated in this way because they give enough support to the larger and heavier bench plane. Bench planes have a certain amount of weight and mass and this weight is valuable in driving the plane through the cut. It may be necessary for you to plane in from both sides, but if that is not possible take a small 45° paring or backing cut at the end to help prevent breakout.

Using a block plane

For smaller components it is possible to use a block plane (see page 17) on end grain. This is a small plane used with one hand, which is specially designed for use on end grain lumber. The block plane is designed with a very low cutting angle of between 13° and 19°. Many planes of this type have an adjustable mouth. This should be set very close to the blade, probably no more than 1/64 inch (0.4 mm) away from the end of the cutting iron. Unlike bench planes, block planes are honed and sharpened with the edge straight across rather than slightly rounded, thus a shaving made with a block plane is a shaving created using the full width of the blade. Set the block plane with a sharp, well-honed iron set to cut a fine shaving and you will find that planing end grain becomes straightforward and pleasant work.

Using a shooting board

For planing small components, a jig called a shooting board is a useful bench accessory, and can be made in the workshop or

Above *Sawn end grain prior to being planed*

Above *A cut angled at 45° to prevent breakout on the end of a board*

bought from a manufacturer. Clamp the shooting board to the bench top. Place the job on top and hold it against a stop at one end of the shooting board. Then run the bench plane along the length of the shooting board on its side, at a right angle to the job. In this way, small components can be trimmed extremely accurately and with great control. Shooting boards can be used for planing both with and across the grain. When using one across the grain, be careful not to extend the job too far beyond the support piece, otherwise breakout will occur if you plane through the work. Shooting boards are especially useful for working on small components, probably less than 15¾ inches (400 mm) in length.

USING A BENCH PLANE

1 Before using a bench plane to finish the end grain on a large board, first set up the component vertically in a vise.

2 The plane blade needs to be sharp and finely set.

3 Use a shooting board to cut and square end grain or for planing long narrow edges.

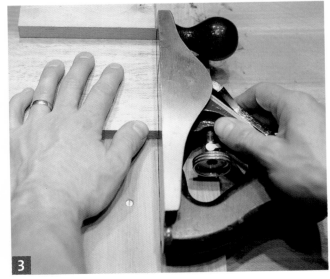

Machining to length

MUCH OF THE MARKING and cutting of joints is carried out with the material slightly longer than finished size, but there comes a time when components have to be accurately dimensioned and cut to length. There are various workshop machine tools that can be used to perform this task. However, it is perfectly possible to undertake this operation by hand, using the sawing and end planing techniques shown previously.

Crosscutting with saws
TABLE SAW A table saw is the most commonly used machine for sawing a component to length. It is essential that a table saw is firstly set up square in both directions. A small all-metal engineer's square is best used to check that the saw blade is exactly at right angles to the table of the machine, and that the miter gauge is also running at a true 90° to the blade. Alternatively, you could check this against a perfectly planed square piece of MDF. When you use the miter gauge it is common practice first to attach a false fence. This is trimmed by the blade of the table saw and then provides a perfect reference surface for locating your job on the miter gauge or sliding table fence. It tells you exactly where the saw will cut and also provides back-up to the job, helping to prevent breakout at the back of the cut.

BAND SAW Crosscutting can also be done on the band saw. If it is set up correctly, this can be a very accurate machine, but

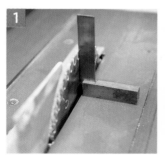

USING A TABLE SAW

1 Check that the saw blade is at 90° to the table surface, and that the sliding fence is at 90° to the blade.

2 Fix a false fence to the crosscut sliding fence.

3 Trim it to make a good reference surface for your work.

4 The trimmed fence indicates where the saw will make its cut.

the surface of the cut is slightly coarser than that produced by the table saw. Set up the miter gauge and the relationship of the blade to the machine table in exactly the same way as with a table saw. If you trim the component slowly and carefully, you can achieve highly accurate and clean work using a band saw.

RADIAL ARM SAW The radial arm saw is a common machine in commercial workshops but is found less often in the home workshop. It is included here because it is designed as a crosscutting saw. With this machine, the saw is drawn across the job and cuts through not only the rear fence but also very slightly into the table upon which the job is supported. Because the blades used on radial arm saws are specifically designed for crosscutting, you tend to get a very fine finish straight from the saw. If you want, radial arm saws can also be used with a stop on the back fence to enable a number of components to be cut to a predetermined length.

Other crosscutting machines

It is not necessary to have large machines to trim components to length. A circular saw and a router can also be used for this task. You will need to clamp a straight scrap of wood at right angles across your job and to guide the saw or the router using that fence. This technique is especially useful when cutting dadoes across the insides of carcasses to accept shelving components.

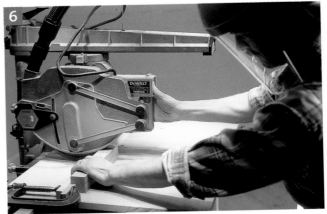

USING A BAND SAW

5 You can also use a band saw to cut across the grain, ensuring before use that the band saw, too, is set up accurately at 90° to the machining table.

USING A RADIAL ARM SAW

6 Crosscutting is also possible with a radial arm saw.

USING A ROUTER

7 Another option is to use a plunge router to groove across the grain.

The router as the main shop tool

A SMALL ¼-inch (6-mm) plunge router is one of the most versatile power tools that a woodworker can possess these days. It can be used easily to dimension lumber, to cut joints, and to decorate and create moldings. The most important aspect is the accuracy provided by using a router. Routed surfaces are dead square, dead flat and perfectly accurate.

A router can be used in many ways as a the main shop tool, doing the job of many of the tools or machines that you do not already possess. It can function like a saw, creating truly straight edges at perfect right angles to a face side. For this, you need nothing more complicated than a long guide fence, which can be placed on your job at an equal distance from the edge that you wish to plane and cut dead straight and true.

Another feature of the router is that it can create a curved surface, simply by being guided along a curved rather than a straight fence. (The curved template can be created using a band saw and finished using a compass plane or spokeshave.) This curved template or fence can then be used to create a number of curved components, each with exactly the same curve routed upon them.

Once you have your face edge, you can create a parallel surface using the side fence provided with the router. This guides the cutter along a line you determine exactly parallel with the existing face edge. For work of this kind it is best to use a straight cutter of suitable size. Never plunge and cut more than

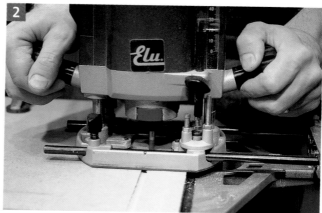

How a router works

A router spins in one direction, so you need to ensure that you always have the router bit turning into the edge of the material that you are cutting or molding. In this way the fence of the router will be pulled up against the edge rather than being pushed away.

Right *View from above of a router in use*

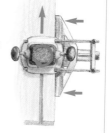

USING FENCES

1 Using a router with a curved fence to make repeatable curved shapes.

2 Cutting a groove using the router's own side fence.

ROUTER CUTTERS

3 A router cutter with a guide bearing *in situ*.

4 This guide bearing guides the cutter against the edge of the board to cut a rabbet.

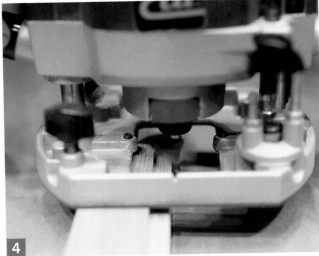

bearing. This guide bearing runs against the part of the wood beneath the rabbet and guides the cutter. It is not good practice to run a rabbet of this kind all at one cut; instead, make two passes, the second pass being a fine, light, cleaning-up cut.

You could create the same rabbet using a simple straight cutter and the side fence that was provided with the router. In this case the side fence would be running against the edge of your job.

Dadoes can be created relatively easily by setting up a router with a suitably sized straight bit, and setting up a long fence in a suitable position, parallel with the gauge marks of the dado, and then guiding the router against this fence.

Mortising is usually done with a mortising machine (see page 68), but failing that, a

the diameter of your cutter. So, if you are using a ⁵⁄₁₆-inch (8-mm) diameter straight bit, you would cut ³⁄₄-inch (20-mm) wood using three passes. If routing an edge as described above, it is best to first trim it to within sight of your line, using a handsaw or a band saw, and

then to finish off the cut with the router, rather than attempting to clear a lot of waste and create much dust and noise using your router.

Rabbets, dadoes and mortises

Rabbets can be cut away using a router cutter fitted with a guide router can be used to cut small mortises. This is easily achieved on relatively wide stock, but on narrow stock it is often necessary to pad out the sides of the rail with a piece of scrap wood on either side. This gives a suitable supportive platform upon which the router stands. The router can then be guided off the side of components using the side fence provided with the router.

Moldings

One of the most common uses for a router is in creating moldings. This can be done using a wide range of cutters, creating decorative shapes and forms – from a simple rounding-over cutter to a decorative and classic ogee. Cutters are guided either by the side fence or workshop-made template or jig, or by a bearing or pin situated on the cutter itself. Occasionally, a decorative cutter will have two sizes of bearing. This effectively enables the cutter to cut two moldings from one cutter. Large scribe and stick molding cutters are sold in pairs, most commonly for molding the frame of frame-and-panel kitchen doors. These create a molding around the door and also create the joint between the stile and rails. Since these are relatively large cutters, a large router is recommended for use with them, preferably one that has a ½-inch (13-mm) collet and is table mounted.

5

6

The router table

Routers can be used in various ways upside down in a router table. This enables the work to be taken to the router rather than the other way round. Bear in mind when using a router table that the direction of the rotation of the cutter is reversed and work should be fed into the cutter, usually from the right-hand side. Router tables are especially useful when molding or machining small components. You do not have to buy a commercially made router table since you can easily make one in the workshop that will probably function far better than those that are commercially available.

ROUTING MORTISES

5 Cutting a mortise on a reasonably wide component.

6 If the component is narrow, use some waste stock on both sides to give a suitable platform.

ROUTING RABBETS

7 Cutting a rabbet using the router's side fence.

USING A ROUTER TABLE

8 A router inverted under a router table, showing the projecting cutter and the safety guards.

9 Feeding the component over the router cutter against the side fence, with the hold-down providing downward pressure.

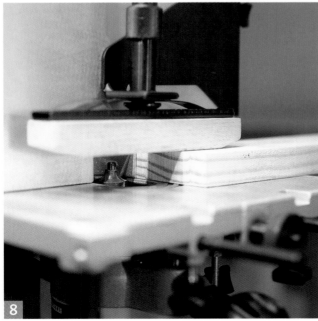

Drilling and mortising

A FREQUENT OPERATION in woodworking is to make various sizes and types of holes in assorted components in order to make certain joints, fix various fittings such as door catches, and so on. Simple hand tools can often be used, although hand-held power tools and machines are particularly useful for making repetitive joints such as a mortise-and-tenon joint.

Drilling

Many of the light woodworking processes can be carried out using hand tools, and one of the most useful is the hand drill and twist drill. The drill is inserted into the chuck, which is tightened by hand. You need to mark accurately where the holes are needed, ideally marking the center of the proposed hole with an awl or a punch, since twist drills need this location point when the hole is started. If you have many small holes to drill, a light electric drill is useful, preferably battery-operated, which offers more flexibility in the way you approach the work.

If you have a lot of holes to drill, a most useful machine tool is a drill press, either bench or floor mounted. These usually have a range of speeds to suit various materials and drills, and can accept adapter kits, including a mortising attachment and sanding drums.

Most operations can now be carried out with the above tools, but larger holes were originally cut using a hand brace with a series of bits. These are still useful in the workshop, especially if your range of machine tools is limited.

Mortising

A mortise machine is the most common tool for making square holes or mortises. A mortise bit is effectively an

DRILLING BY HAND

1 With the work held in the vise, ensure that the wheelbrace and twist drill are at the correct angle before drilling.

Position yourself so that you are looking directly down over the work in a straight line. Turn the handle, ensuring that when starting to cut, the center of the drill remains in the correct position on the work.

2 A simple depth stop is made by wrapping some masking tape around the drill bit.

DRILL PRESS

3 A drill press in use with its guard in place.

auger surrounded by a square, hollow chisel. The auger cuts slightly ahead of the chisel, and the four corners of the chisel pare out the square corners after the central circle has been removed. In order to use this machine, a considerable amount of downward support has to be exerted to pare out the four corners. This is why mortise machines have very long handles to give added leverage to the downward pull. However, if you pull too hard and force the mortise bit to cut into the lumber too quickly, this causes waste to clog up inside the cutter, driving the center point offline and causing overheating and burning. Mortises therefore need to be cut steadily but firmly.

Mortising bits need to be sharpened with great care. A reamer especially designed for the brand of cutter is set up with a metal plug that fits on to the end of the reamer and also fits the size of chisel being used. The reamer sharpens the inside of the chisel and is used in a hand-operated drill. It should not need too much pressure. The outside of the chisel needs to be honed and the cutting surfaces of the auger should be filed and stoned.

MORTISER ADAPTER KITS

Adapter kits can be purchased for drill presses, which allow the drill press to function as a mortising machine. These function relatively well but can be slow and fiddly to use.

A drill press or a conventional electric drill fitted into a drill stand is a very useful piece of equipment that allows a drill to be presented to the work at 90° and a cut to be taken to a pre-determined depth. Always make sure that a guard is present on a drill press and always be careful to take the chuck key out of the chuck when a piece of tooling is removed.

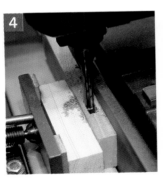

MORTISING MACHINE

4 A mortising machine in action, showing the chisel making a cut in work that is securely held by waste stock and a clamp.

5 Detail showing the auger within the square hollow chisel of the mortise bit.

HORIZONTAL MORTISING

6 Another way of creating mortises is to use a horizontal mortiser, whereby a slot mortiser cuts the mortises effectively.

Shaping

CURVED SHAPES and components can be created in a variety of ways. It has already been described how a router can be used to make these (see page 64), but there are other power tools that can help put the curves into your woodworking.

Shaping with saws

Unless you buy a particularly powerful jigsaw, you will find yourself limited to working with thin boards or wood of a thickness of 1 inch (25 mm) or less. Although, technically, a jigsaw will cut a thickness of more than 1 inch, it will not do so very accurately. The jigsaw is mostly used to rough out a shape, probably cutting just slightly shy of your guideline.

Scroll saws are much more involved pieces of equipment. An intricate design can be worked using a scroll saw and, because of the fineness of the blade, the surface created is of a polished and burnished nature. Quite often, scroll saws slightly burn and blacken the wood as they cut, but it is usual not to attempt to clean up the surface left by this saw.

Band saws are extremely versatile for curved work. You are limited only by the throat of your band saw and by the size of the band-saw blade. Quite often, a relatively large band saw will take a very small ¼-inch (6-mm) band, which will enable you to cut tight curves. The table of the band saw can be tilted should you wish to cut a curve at a 45° angle or less, and compound curves within intricate shapes can be created.

A band saw or a jigsaw will usually saw a shape shy of a marked line. To finish to the line, your options are either to use hand tools such as spokeshaves or compass planes, or to use a spindle sander fitted in a drill press. The spindle sander will give the component a clean, curved surface at 90° to its face side. Hand tools such as spokeshaves and compass planes require considerably more skill to operate as they will be cutting into and out of the grain of the wood and so demand great awareness of the material by the craftsperson.

SHAPING COMPONENTS USING SAWS

1 The jigsaw is a useful tool for cutting curves prior to cleaning up the cut edges.

2 Very fine curves can be cut using a scroll saw.

3 Similarly, the band saw can be used for cutting curves, and the angle of the band-saw table can be tilted to provide more shaping options.

4 Spindle sanders are available in several different diameters. The one shown here is used in a drill press to finish band-sawn components.

SHAPING WITH A SANDER

5 A bench-mounted belt-and-disc combination sander can be used to shape components once the bulk of the waste has been removed with a saw. Here a convex curve is being shaped and sanded.

6 Sanding the concave face of a component against the end roller of a belt sander.

7 Using a disc sander with table and miter gauge to trim to precise angles for miter joints.

Wood Species of the World

OUR ENVIRONMENT is dominated by different species of trees that we probably take for granted, and wood is utilized in such complex ways that it is now an integral part of everyday life. It is only when we explore this living material that we enter a fascinating world of subtlety and find an infinite variety of patterns and colors. The following pages illustrate just some of the vast range of species available.

Softwoods

The term "non-porous" is sometimes applied by botanists to softwood species. These are coniferous trees, and many of them grow in the northern hemisphere. Instead of moisture passing through open cells throughout the tree's length, as in hardwoods, each individual softwood cell relies on moisture passing through its cell wall. This often causes softwoods to perform quite differently than hardwoods when used in the workshop.

Parana pine
Araucaria angustifolia
The joy of this pine is that it is generally knot free, often growing above 70ft (21m) in height. It is used for internal work where the reddish streaks are regarded as a feature.

Scotch pine
Pinus sylvestris
In Western Europe this species abounds as household furniture and structural members in house building. Its wide summer growth is quite soft, making the harder winter growth pronounced. It changes color with ultraviolet light.

Cedar of Lebanon
Cedrus libani
A general term, since there are three or four different cedars of similar characteristics. This species is famous for its strong fragrance, which deters moths, and is often used as a drawer lining. It is very light with little constructional strength, but much sought after for small boxes and caskets.

Douglas fir
Pseudotsuga taxifolia
A giant of a tree, often growing in excess of 280 feet (85 m). Generally reddish in color, the sectional sizes available are enormous; thus its use is vast, from large wooden structures to interior usages. Not only is it very tough but also water resistant.

Larch
Larix decidua
A wonderful wood for outdoor use, it not only grows to great height but produces really wide boards. Often seen in the form of fences, garden sheds and even flooring in outdoor and indoor buildings. Unlike the pines and spruces, which are evergreen, this species loses its leaves in winter.

Yew
Taxus baccata
Some trees exceed 1,000 years in age. Yew has extraordinary elastic properties, hence its historical use for long bows and Windsor chairs. The foliage is poisonous to many animals, including cattle.

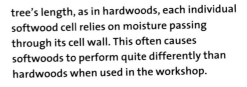

Western red cedar
Thuja plicata

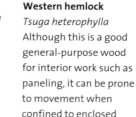

A real giant of a tree, available in wide boards and very easy to work. The lovely scent can remain in the wood, especially when used in confined spaces. Very durable and much used for internal joinery. Especially good for building houses as it withstands almost any climatic conditions.

Western hemlock
Tsuga heterophylla

Although this is a good general-purpose wood for interior work such as paneling, it can be prone to movement when confined to enclosed temperature-variable conditions. It grows fast, is very clean and even in grain, and is sometimes called fir or spruce.

Hardwoods

From early experiments it has been discovered which woods are durable and perform well, for tool-, ship- and furniture-making, even wheel-making. In these categories hardwoods (broad-leaved trees that mostly lose their leaves in winter), generally perform better than softwoods. This may well be due, in part, to the different composition of the cell structure in hardwoods, which allows much greater flexibility than in most softwoods.

Sycamore
Acer pseudoplatanus

Although beautifully white when converted, in time it turns yellowish brown. In quartered boards the medullary rays are beautiful and very subtle. The boards must be stood on end to season or the color is lost forever. A superb wood once tamed.

Alder
Alnus glutinosa

An unusual wood in that it has almost no use in furniture-making because of its wild nature on exposure to air. Below ground it is imperishable, but if you are offered any, observe its wild erratic shrinkage and politely decline!

Sugar maple
Acer saccharum

This species comes from Canada and, like most maples, is very versatile: from furniture-making to fine letter blocks for the printing trade, to tool handles and billiard cues. It ages and discolors less than sycamore and its grain can be very wavy.

Zebrano
Brachystegia fleuryana

This is another exotic wood, which offers a range of colors in the form of stripes. Zebrano is often used as a detail in marquetry but its initial luster can fade when exposed to too much ultraviolet light.

Box

Buxus sempervirens
One of those woods to which every furniture-maker must turn. It is close grained, with a pale straw-yellowish color. You will find it only in small sections, but do buy it. Even in small inlay strips it is beautifully hard and provides great protection for vulnerable corners and edges.

Hornbeam

Carpinus betulus
A wood with engineering qualities in that it can produce wooden screws. Heavy and very tough, it is not commercially readily available. Its great use is for tool parts, such as plane stocks, and where a shaped block can be worked on, as in the leather trade.

Sweet chestnut

Castanea sativa
Sometimes called "poor man's oak" because of its resemblance to flat sawn oak. Softer than oak but found in larger sections. Although few medullary rays are seen, this wood is delightful to work. Its high tannic acid content stains fingers very easily.

Iroko

Chlorophora excelsa
A pale to dark-brown wood, not unlike to teak in appearance. It is a nightmare to machine without good dust-collection facilities as its pungent smell irritates the nasal passages. A good outdoor wood for garden furniture and sites where humidity levels change.

Bubinga

Copaifera amoldiana
A West African hardwood, available in veneer and solid form. A fairly dense wood, which is reddy brown with dark thin lines giving an interesting pattern, often seen when used for the manufacture of plywood. Sometimes this species is known as kevazingo.

Rosewood

Dalbergia
There are various rosewoods: Rio, Indian, East Indian, British Honduras, etc. For some years source countries have imposed an export ban so it is difficult to obtain. Difficult to glue and prone to fine surface splits, but equally an amazingly beautiful wood.

Kingwood

Dalbergia cearensis
A very striking wood from Brazil, which is difficult to obtain in anything other than small sections. It is often sold not by cubic content but by weight. A dense wood that polishes well and is often seen as decoration in a piece of furniture.

Tulipwood

Dalbergia oliveri
Confusingly called "poplar" by some lumber suppliers. It is not, and its source is Myanmar (formerly Burma). A very dense wood, used and sold in a similar way to kingwood. In the USA the tulip tree is likely to be called poplar – though of different appearance to this species.

Cocobolo

Dalbergia retusa
So difficult to obtain and very
expensive. Beautiful to turn,
but inclined
to have an interlocked
spiral grain, which
makes planing difficult.

Jarrah

Eucalyptus marginata
One of the commonest trees of
the southwest United States,
jarrah is a strong wood
suitable for outdoor use .
Also used for internal
cabinet work, it has a very even
red color.

Macassar ebony

Diospyros macassar
Rich and streaky, especially in
veneer form. A dense wood,
ranging in color from yellow to
deep brown with dark stripes.
The grain is so powerfully
stripy that it can overpower the
overall shape of the furniture. In wall panels, or
tables it can be very bold.

Mountain ash

Eucalyptus regnans
Not a true ash but an Australian
eucalyptus, this can have a
number of different names –
Tasmanian oak, Australian
oak, giant gum, white ash.
Grows to a very large size, but is
likely to resist even drying and, because of its
fast growth rate, can be liable to distortion.

Jelutong

Dyera costulata
Sometimes called "jelly" in the
trade, this pale-yellow lumber
is excellent to veneer on.
Very stable but dull in
appearance. An annoying
trait is the many worm holes
combined with oval-shaped resin pockets that
can break out over the planed board.

European beech

Fagus sylvatica
An excellent wood to steam
bend, solid beech is known
for moving and shrinking.
This shrinkage is 400
percent greater than any
other comparable hardwood in
Europe. However, it can work beautifully when dry,
and woodworking tools are often made of beech.

Sapele mahogany

Entandrophragma cylindricum
Very stripy lumber that,
because of the size of the
tree, appears in very wide
boards. When converted
into veneered panels and
seen *en masse*, it is not very
exciting. Used by piano makers and in
commercially produced doors.

European ash

Fraxinus excelsior
A confusing name, as it is also
called peppermint ash and
giant gum ash. In Europe it
is known as olive ash,
generally occurring after
30 years' growth when the
white heart has turned to streaky olive. Springy, it
is good for sports equipment (i.e., archery bows).

Ramin

Gonystylus macrophyllum
One of a family of similar trees
from Southeast Asia. Very
open, featureless straight-
grained wood that is hard
to cut to a crisp finish.
Splinters are poisonous and
must be removed from the skin immediately. Used
for door and window frames and making plywood.

American whitewood

Liriodendron tulipifera
Second rate in its use for
furniture, but excellent as a
good stable sub-base or
where painted furniture is
required. It machines easily
and is excellent for making jigs.
It is confusingly called tulipwood poplar, and some
lumber dealers even call it tulipwood.

Lignum vitae

Guaiacum officinale
Another lumber sold by weight
and one that sinks in water. It
has an oily texture, which
makes gluing difficult. It's
used for making mallets
and bowling balls but is not
suitable for furniture-making.

Wenge

Millettia laurentii
Planed boards will change in
ultraviolet light from straw to
almost black. Open pored
but, with a good grain
filler, replaces rosewood
admirably. Very straight
grained, but for small areas such as turnings it has
a wonderful grain distinction. Brittle and splintery.

American black walnut

Juglans nigra
A beautiful wood, perhaps more
in the burr veneer form than
in the slightly plain solid
form. Although easy to
work it can prove less
exciting than its European
counterpart. Regardless of aesthetics, however,
this is a magnificent furniture-making wood.

Balsa wood

Ochroma lagopus
A confusing wood: the lightest
wood in the world and the
softest, yet classified as a
hardwood! A marvelous
wood for model-making
and for containers requiring
buoyancy.

European walnut

Juglans regia
Without doubt, this wood's
ease of usage, color, texture,
figure and sheer depth of
beauty, combined with
stability and its vast range
of applications, from turning
to furniture, make this one species that has to be
experienced.

Olive

Olea hochstetteri
A very stripy and powerful grain
is attributed to this dense
species, which comes mainly
from Kenya. It is often used
in the production of small
decorative items and burr
olive is a real delight to
the eye.

Plane (lacewood)

Platanus acerifolia
A species that, when the
medullary rays are seen in the
quartered board, is known
as lacewood. The tree is
predominant in many
cities and is distinguished by
its peeling bark. A good furniture wood with
great subtlety.

Padauk

Pterocarpus dalbergiodes
Not too dissimilar to muninga.
It is difficult to work because
of its interlocked surface,
but if you persevere your
reward will be a beautiful
rich, deep-red wood with dark
streaks dancing over the surface. The color fades
somewhat when exposed to ultraviolet light.

English cherry

Prunus avium
Often a difficult wood to
obtain. It can be difficult to
plane without tear-out,
especially on quartered
boards, but the close
grain can polish beautifully.

American white oak

Quercus alba
This oak is regarded by many as
adequate in that it is durable
and tough, has good
sectional sizes and length,
but is prone to having
sapwood included in sawn
boards. It is, however, dull and must rank as a
functional oak rather than a character oak.

American cherry

Prunus serotina
Difficult to obtain in good
quality outside the United
States as it is rarely
exported. High degree of
sapwood on each board,
and board conversion for
maximum volume, mean most exported stock has
excessive movement and wastage is high.

American red oak

Quercus borealis/rubra
One could argue that whereas
there is a greater depth of
color to red oak, compared
with white oak, its main
disadvantage (to some) is
that it cannot take stain
readily. A very similar wood in working qualities to
that of white oak.

Muninga

Pterocarpus angolensis
Not always easy to obtain but
freely available in southern
Africa. It is a very versatile
wood and has the
advantage of being
resistant to decay.

English oak

Quercus robur
The English oak has a majesty
all of its own and, of all
the oaks, is the most
magnificent for
furniture-making.

Brazilian mahogany

Swietenia macrophylla

Although this species is the best available mahogany from any of the exporting countries, our obligation to our environment and to world conservation principles means trying to use mahoganies from other sources where conservation is an important factor.

Teak

Tectona grandis

A wood that exudes a natural oil from its pores, enabling it to withstand exceptional conditions. Very difficult to degrease for gluing purposes, but still a joy to work despite its calcium pockets and grit particles blunting your tools. Excellent for furniture-makers.

Indian laurel

Terminalia tomentosa

A species that can resemble walnut to a degree. It shows strong, generally straight grain in solid form, but in veneer form it can be very highly figured. Very open pored and requires filling to obtain a good finish.

European lime

Tilia vulgaris

One of only a very few woods, but arguably the best, for carving. The world's greatest carvings are generally in lime, which is a real delight to work. Unfortunately not really suitable for furniture.

Obeche

Triplochiton scleroxylon

A very good wood for drawer bases, partitions, rails that require veneering, and so on. This pale straw-colored wood is useful as a good stable base to be incorporated with other woods.

British elm

Ulmus procera

A pity this is so prone to Dutch elm disease. When available, this magnificent species provides all that one could want for durability, size, depth of beauty and wonderfully exotic figure.

Index

Acknowledgments

The publishers would like to thank the following for their assistance in supplying equipment and materials for the book:

Alan Holtham, Cheshire

Axminster Power Tool Centre, Axminster, Devon

Crown Hand Tools Ltd, Sheffield, Yorkshire

Elu Power Tools Ltd, Slough, Berkshire

Foxell & James Ltd, London

J Crispins & Son, London

JSM Joinery, London

Morgans of Strood, Strood, Kent

Parry Tyzack, London

Peter Child, Essex

Racal Health & Safety Ltd, Greenford, Middlesex

Wilson Bros., Northfleet, Kent

The publishers and photographers would like to thank all the contributors for their patient help and advice. Special thanks go to Mark Ripley for his skills and imagination, and clear demonstrations of techniques. Thanks also to the following for their help on location shoots: Gordon Stone, Paul Mitchard, Graham Mills, Gurk, Darren Francis, John Ingram, John Taylor and Mick O'Donnell.

All photography by Colin Bowling and Paul Forrester for Hamlyn.

Editorial Manager: Jane Birch

Senior Designer: Claire Harvey

Project Manager: Jo Lethaby

Designer: Mark Stevens

Picture Researcher: Christine Junemann

Senior Production Controller: Louise Hall